BLUE FLARE
Three Haitian Poets

Évelyne Trouillot
Marie-Célie Agnant
Maggy de Coster

Translated from the French and Kreyòl by
Danielle Legros Georges

ZEPHYR PRESS

This publication is made possible in part by the Academy of American
Poets with funds from the Amazon Literary Partnership Poetry Fund.

Zephyr Press acknowledges with gratitude the financial support of the
Massachusetts Cultural Council.

Zephyr Press, a non-profit arts and education 501(c)(3) organization,
publishes literary titles that foster a deeper understanding of cultures
and languages. Zephyr Press books are distributed to the trade by
Consortium Book Sales and Distribution [www.cbsd.com].

Cataloging-in-publication data is available from the Library of Congress.

ZEPHYR PRESS
www.zephyrpress.org

Table of Contents

Blue Flare: Three Haitian Poets

Danielle Legros Georges

In Haitian popular culture, women have long been called *poto mitan,* or middle posts of families and of the society at large. The metaphor is meant to flatter, comparing the domestic and infrastructural roles women often occupy with the vertical weight-bearing beams of *hounfours,* or vodou temples. A temple's *poto mitan* is the essential and central pole from which other beams extend horizontally to create a sheltered space. At times, the pole is a tree through which the gods descend to commune with and inhabit the living within a vodou cosmological framework and its rituals. Without the *poto mitan,* there would be no *hounfour,* no spiritual center. In addition to its religious basis the term *poto mitan* can evoke a broader public context of nationalism, which often compels the sublimation of one's individuality for perceived broader social goals.

The *poto mitan* trope has been critiqued by some Haitian feminists for rendering invisible the difficult choices made by women to negotiate and survive the constructs that impact and at times cast shadows over their lives. These include state-based gender discrimination and violence, and the chronic political instability in Haiti. The metaphor recognizes women's social contributions but cannot account for the nuanced experiences and strategies that give shape, meaning, and beauty to female lives. Here is where Haitian women writers step in, or *write* in.

As a writer and a translator, I have attempted to locate and explore terrains through and beyond the sway of *poto mitan* exigencies, not merely as a reactionary gesture but for the visions and incarnations of important truths and full humanities found thereon.

The two women who raised me, my mother and paternal grandmother, while overburdened with familial responsibility, saw themselves neither as *poto mitan* nor as voiceless victims of their circumstances. *Au contraire.* Their lives were full—of many things, some in seeming contradiction. I became a writer in part to crack open the *au contraires*, particularly those rendered complex by emigration from Haiti and displacement's many challenges and opportunities. I sought, as they had, to manage the spaces between burdened and empowered.

Language and art-making served as powerful sites of investigation of the relationship between burdened and empowered, between responsibility and freedom. Language and art-making led me to poetry; and later, to the literary translation of poetry, beginning with the work of the Haitian-French poet Ida Faubert, whose 1939 *Cœur des îles* beckoned me with its evidence of Faubert's formal precision as a poet, unusual biography, and place in Haitian letters as a significant foremother. My Faubert translation project culminated in the 2021 publication of *Island Heart: Poems of Ida Faubert* (Subpress) and led to my desire to translate more Haitian women poets from whom I knew I could learn much; this especially since so few Francophone and Kreyòlophone texts written by them existed in English.

In addition to a desire to read and study Haitian women poets through the occasion that translation provided, I was, and am, interested in texts whose themes tackle colonial legacies, neocolonial or postcolonial challenges, and which signal a general commitment to issues of social justice. Moreover, as a translator, I am drawn to approaches to, and obstacles that may present themselves in, the rendering of texts from cultures and spaces already bicultural, or multilingual and multicultural—such as Haiti, the Caribbean, and African diasporic spaces more broadly. Translating Haitian women allows me to attend to both personal and social principles, and to the political questions I feel are inherent to the act and publication of translation.

The first writer whose poems were translated for this book was Marie-Célie Agnant, whom I had the good fortune of meeting in 1996 while a graduate student at New York University. Agnant's New York visit included a marvelous reading from *Balafres,* her then-recently-published first book whose gravitas struck me, as did her commanding presence. While I was aware of Haitian writers of my generation, I had yet to meet an established Haitian woman activist and *poet* with as serious a commitment to a writing life as Agnant made visible. Her inscription to my copy of *Balafres,* (*de poètesse à poetèsse, de femme a femme . . .*), sealed a deal I made then to study Agnant's poetic ouvre.

My meeting with the noted Évelyne Trouillot was facilitated by a 2015 trip to Haiti. There to conduct writing workshops with Haitian university and high school students, I met Trouillot on the grounds of the Centre Culturel Anne-Marie Morisset, the non-profit organization she founded with her siblings. The Centre, located in the Delmas 41 neighborhood, was buzzing with young people, reflecting its mission to contribute to the cultural development of Haitian youth in general, and in Delmas in particular. After I'd conducted a workshop with a lively group, Trouillot invited me into the Centre's library where she generously presented me with several books including *Plidetwal,* a beautiful surprise as I hadn't been aware that she wrote poems in Kreyòl. Of course, I read it on my return trip. Of course, I made a note to begin translating her beautiful long poem.

Finally, with the Agnant and Trouillot translations almost complete in 2022, and with the possibility of a publisher for these translations, I sought a third Haitian woman poet with a book written in a language other than English to establish a triptych, and what I hoped would be a fruitful experience for readers presented with texts of unique and varying sensibilities.

A number of the Haitian women poets I admired (many of them my Haitian-American contemporaries) already had published books of poetry in English. My search for a third poet brought into view Maggy de Coster's long career as both a journalist and writer. Our first and felicitous meeting took place over Zoom at the end of 2022; she in Paris, me in Boston, grateful for the unifying power of technology.

Blue Flare: Three Haitian Poets represents the first English translations of selected works by these three celebrated writers who confront and contend with the complexity of life in Haiti and its diaspora in the 21st century. Writing from the standpoints of, and attending to, the lived experiences of women, Évelyne Trouillot, Marie-Célie Agnant, and Maggy de Coster present readers with texts that reveal and dream, that instigate interrogations, that move beyond the ground of the nationalistic, that express deep commitments to questions of ethics, that mine intersections and occupy crossroads.

Trouillot's *Plidetwal (Rain of Stars),* written in Haitian, or Kreyòl, was published in Port-au-Prince by Édition Presses Nationales d'Haïti, Collection Souffle Nouveau in 2005. Opening with the question "in what language should I speak to you?" the book's speaker engages a singular beloved, the other, as well as a beloved country in which night sits at the front door "even at sunrise." A desire for dialogue pulses through the poems which ask us to consider our current relationships and tensions of great precarity and great love. Where do we place ourselves? In this image-rich, deeply figurative book, Trouillot also explores the possible limits of language.

Trouillot lives in Port-au-Prince, where she is a retired professor of the French department of the Université d'État d'Haïti. She is the author of four collections of short stories, two volumes of stories for children, four books of poems, an award-winning play, and eight novels including *Rosalie l'infâme (The Infamous*

Rosalie), which received the 2004 Prix de la romancière francophone du Club Soroptimist de Grenoble. Her works have been translated into English, German, Italian, Portuguese, and Spanish. A member of one of Haiti's most fertile intellectual and literary families, Trouillot stands alongside her siblings: novelist and poet Lyonel Trouillot; anthropologist, historian, and social scientist Michel-Rolph Trouillot; and Kreyòl scholar and children's book author Jocelyne Trouillot. She is the co-founder of Pré-Texte, a writer's organization that sponsors readings and writing workshops.

To translate *Plidetwal* into English required a recognition of the already highly figurative nature of the Haitian language. We Haitians are known for the everyday poetry and sophisticated word play in our interactions with each other, facilitated by Kreyòl; and for proverbs: networks of metaphors that help illuminate the political, economic, social, familial, and other situations we all find ourselves in. Many proverbs are rooted in Haitian oral culture and echo the incisive comparative and inventive abilities of their authors, often ancient and unidentified poets. I had to determine, for example, which images and image-systems were Trouillot's, and which were grounded in Kreyòl. In the poem "Peyi m" ("My Country"), Trouillot draws a contrast between Haiti and a place where life doles out sparkles and where "machin ponn lajan," where "machines lay money," as birds may lay eggs. I knew immediately what was meant but did not know if the expression was a familiar one. In the end (or in the beginning), the image was Trouillot's, reflecting her inventive (and delightful) comparison of hens and ATMs.

Another kind of challenge presented itself in how, or if, to translate particular Haitian (and also Afro-diasporic) practices and experiences—such as that of *plim poul* for the Anglophone (and Western) reader who may never have had a chicken feather inserted into her ear, and twisted this way and that to produce a most pleasant sensation. Because I have chosen not to interpolate lengthy explanations into the lines of poetry, the preceding explanation did not make its way into the translation of the following passage: "Se te yon fwa / Yon lang ki fè pye m leje / Li pase plim poul sou tout anvi m," which appears thus "There was once / A tongue that made my feet light / That tickled all my desires."

Agnant's *Balafres (Gashes)*, written in French and published in Montréal by Éditions du CIDIHCA in 1994, enfolds poems that traverse time and space. It is the first volume of poems and first book written by Agnant, an introduction of the many themes she will employ and elaborate in her subsequent work. These include hybridity, the transmission of memory against the backdrop of exile and displacement, the narratives of Haitian and Black girls and women, the effects of dictatorship and colonialism, the bearing of witness, and questions of voice and interventions against silence. In *Balafres*, Agnant articulates the need to write "all the complicit silences." The volume's first poem conjures the ancient Greek female chthonic deities, to whom the poem's speaker draws a comparison—signaling in "Eumenides" a temporal gateway and feminist terrain. The poem stands alongside one ("Noon") that addresses the struggle of earthly women who "bury [a] dead child / the dead child in arms / with no flowers no wreaths . . . without knowing why they exist / in the alleys without names / in the cities without names."

Agnant is a writer, translator, and activist whose novels have been widely translated, including *The Book of Emma* (2004), which evokes the hardships endured by enslaved women in the Caribbean and the challenges to giving voice to this history today. Living in Montréal and writing across literary genres, she has produced poetry, fiction, and books for young readers. She received the Prix Alain-Grandbois of the Academie des Lettres du Quebec in 2017 for her most recent collection of poetry, *Femmes des terres brûlées* (2016). Her critically acclaimed work offers poignant refusals of silence. She has worked with Vermont's Bread and Puppet Theatre, and in 2023 was appointed the Canadian Parliamentary Poet Laureate.

The poems of *Balafres* cover much ground: geographical, temporal, and referential. They are also written employing both narrative and lyrical approaches. Some poems contain overtly political messages, others seem to reflect the intensely personal. How to pull the threads together in translation, and to find what I sensed was the heart of Agnant's literary expression and general aesthetic sensibility in this, her first book? In most of the poems, I found a strong speaker with unmistakable opinions, many rooted in feminist principles. Few of Agnant's poems are muted meditations or open-ended descriptions of a distant omniscient narrator. This strength of voice and an accompanying sense of clear purpose seemed important to convey. These dynamics guided me. The poem "Inventaire," for example, begins with the following stanza:

> Fleur Flamme Femme Fontaine
> on t'a voulu vestale
> on t'a voulu flamme
> flamme-vestale femme-forteresse
> pour veiller
> conforter
> donner vie
> aux sexes fragiles
> sexes frimas

The original stanza's penultimate line does not specify a gender with "aux sexes fragiles," yet many of the lines around it do. I read the poem as an examination of patriarchal expectations of women. With this understanding, and because I wanted to avoid the term "sex" in English for gender, I chose to render the term

particular:

> Flower Flame Woman Fountain
> they wanted you vestal
> they wanted you flame
> flame-vestal woman-fortress
> to watch over
> to comfort
> to give life
> to the fragility of men
> to frost

De Coster's *Les versets simplifiés du soleil levant (The Simplified Verses of the Rising Sun)*, published in Paris by Éditions du Cygne in 2017, presents the reader with a series of epigrammatic poems written in French. A number respond, in witness and imperative, to the social violence that surrounds her in France. "March hands up on freedom's road . . . Resist/Break from the crooked mockers / Be like the tree that sinks its roots into the stream / Slaking those thirsty for life's rays," she writes. In other poems, the author turns herself and us inward in existential meditation, in the desire for calm and lucidity: "With orders to think positively / I will sit on the highest mountain."

De Coster is a poet, novelist, and translator who lives in Paris. As a journalist, she has worked for *Journal de l'Ariège* and other European and international newspapers. She is the author of more than thirty-four books in a variety of genres. Her distinctions include the 2024 Association Apulivre award for a commitment to poetry and culture. She founded the association *Manoir des Poètes*, and her poems have been translated into ten languages.

De Coster's were among the most challenging poems to translate for *Blue Flare* because of their elevated use of abstractions, mixed metaphors, and prosaisms—especially in explorations of the realm of the psyche. While short in length, the poems of *Les versets simplifiés du soleil levant* are often extremely dense due to what I see as De Coster's aesthetic of accretion, of quickly layering. Barely had I deconstructed an idea, image, or framework before I was being presented with another.

Because of the density of these poems, and slipping comparisons, I found myself adopting an approach freer than that used for translating Agnant and Trouillot. This in order to make sense of the work, as imbuing the words (or even phrases) with too much power at times resulted in an inability to grasp the general sense of a poem. The following fragment with its references to the military office of a brigadier, and earlier, to blood, evoked a theater of war. Once established, I could replace the brigadier with the image and evocation of bullets to announce the herald:

Ne pas laisser se répandre des libations de sang
Ne pas laisser fleurir des sentences de haine
Mais aux trois coups de brigadier
Laisser entrer le messager en scène
Pour faire allégeance à l'amour

Don't offer libations of blood
Or allow hate's grammar to grow
When the three shots ring out
Let the messenger enter the scene
To pledge allegiance to love

*   *   *

The poetry gathered in *Blue Flare: Three Haitian Poets* joins a growing list of works in English by Haitian women poets— whether originally written in English or *translated* into English.

These include works made by Lenelle Moïse, Marilène Phipps, Michèle Voltaire Marcelin, Gabrielle Civil, Gina Athena Ulysse, Nadine Pinede, Marie Ketsia Theodore-Pharel, Gina Dorcely, Valérie Déus, and Phebus Étienne (who died too soon in 2007, with a manuscript "Chainstitching" still seeking a publisher).

Blue Flare also responds to what writer and translator John Keene notes as the "considerable body of literature by writers from across the African Diaspora that is not regularly or readily being made available in English." Keene's 2016 clarion call, "Translating Poetry, Translating Blackness" serves as a reminder. "Were more black voices translated," he notes "we would have a clearer sense of the connections and commonalities, as well as the differences across the African Diaspora, and better understand an array of regional, national, and hemispheric issues."

Among Haiti's narratives are two well-known and obstinate ones that create a dialectic in the way Haiti is represented beyond its borders: first, Haiti, with its undeniable 1804 revolution; and second, Haiti as "the poorest nation in the Western Hemisphere." These frameworks locate Haiti in the centuries-old past, and outside of time. Between them runs the thread of a third one: that of an amorphous and perilous darkness.

The texts of contemporary Haitian women stand as flares in that perceived peril. While contemporary Haitian women's novels are being translated into a variety of languages, Francophone and Kreyòlophone women's volumes of poems—as worthy of attention for their complexity and how they reflect women's concerns, particularly in the decades after Haiti's Duvalier dictatorship—have not been widely translated.

My hope is that the translations in *Blue Flame* contribute to the power and beauty of Haitian literary texts as they reflect Haitian and human experiences.

ÉVELYNE TROUILLOT

Plidetwal | *A Rain of Stars*

11

Plidetwal

Nan ki lang pou m pale avè w
Lè pawòl anba dra
Pase souf li sou vant mwen

lavi kenbe m nan kè
koule kafe nan memwa m
li pa di m kote lalin bwè dlo

Lè timoun ap kriye
san rete
youn apre lòt mo yo seche
nan pla men m
san yo pa ban m tan pou m batize fènwa

Kwè m si ou vle
mwen pa konn ki sa ou ye
Yon lonbrit ki pèdi kòd li nan mitan liv pwezi
Yon flè choublak ki gen malozye
Yon zwazo ak zèl li mare dèyè do l
Mwen pantan sou ou
san m pa t konnen kilès ou ye
Jodi a bouch ou tètanba
Rèl sa a pi gwo pase doulè w

11

A Rain of Stars

In what language should I speak to you
when the words beneath our sheets
blow over my belly

life has me holding a grudge
pouring coffee on my recollections
not revealing where the moon finds its water

When children cry
and won't stop
one after the other the words dry up
in the palm of my hand
not letting me baptize the dark

Believe me
I don't know what you are:
A navel that's lost its cord in the midst of a poetry book?
A hibiscus flower with a sickly eye?
A bird with its wings pinned to its back?
I was surprised by you
I didn't know who you were
Today your mouth's upturned
This shout, louder than your pain

12

Nan ki lang pou m pale avè w
lè lapriyè met ajenou devan lamizè
Pitit fi n ap monte kap
bò katedral
Yo bouke lave grenn mab
anndan sakristi

Kwè m si ou vle
M pa konn ki jan ou rele
lè yon ti pòv dizan
dezabiye grangou l nan pye Sentàn
chak grenn diri kite yon mak sou po n

13

Van an kabicha pou l fè nou sou
nou pote l sou do
chimen nou kalboso
nan ki lang pou m pale avè w
lè solèy la
bliye wout li

Kwè m si ou vle
m pa sonje sa k fè m pi mal
m kanpe sou pwent pye pou m ranmase zetwal
yo chavire yo pa janm remonte
Lanmou pèdi papye l
            kontinan pa ret anplas
yon jou sovaj na rankontre
san m pa mande ki moun ou ye

12

In what language should I speak to you
when prayer kneels before poverty
and our daughters fly kites
by the cathedral
sick of washing their marbles
in the vestry

Believe me
I don't know your name
when a ten-year-old beggar
undresses his hunger beneath the statue of Saint Anne
each grain of rice leaving a scar on our skin

13

The wind takes a break to make us drunk
we carry it on our backs
our way is rugged
In what language should I speak to you
when the sun loses its way

Believe me
I don't remember what hurts me most
I stand on tiptoe to gather stars
that capsize never to rise again
Love has lost its name
          continents don't remain steady
one wild day we'll meet
without my knowing who you are

14

Detanzantan m monte bato
kou fèy papye ki pa pran lank
yon sanzatann ki pèdi souf
detanzantan m mouri sou do

Foumi wouj kwaze pat yo nan trip nou
Yo maske pòt lanfè
simayen loseyan ak po kann
Se nan goumen n aprann kanpe
Nan ki lang pou m pale avè w
Si pawòl nou poko sispann bwete

Chak joudlan m mete redengòt
pou m resite Tedeyòm
pandan bonnanj mwen ap pran vwal
Chak joudlan
lè anvi pati fè je m koulè lapli
m antre nan foto w pou m pa lage w

15

Kwè m si ou vle
m pa ka di w pouki m renmen w
gendelè
lari a sanble tout malsite l
li blayi l anfas nostalji m
melanje lodè kadav ak te kanèl

Alòkile pwason bò isit
pa sèvi ak dlo
bri zam gen pouvwa metamòfoz

14

From time to time I board a boat
like a sheet of paper that holds no ink
suddenly set adrift
from time to time I die on my back

Red ants cross their arms in our guts
hiding the door of hell
casting cane husk over the sea
It's in fighting we learn to stand
In what language should I speak to you
if our words haven't stopped limping

Every first of the year, I put on a formal coat
to recite the *te deum*
while my soul loses its bearings
Every first of the year,
when the wish to leave turns my eyes the color of rain
I enter your photo to not let you go

15

Believe me
I can't tell you why I love you
sometimes
The street gathers up all its misery
spreading it in front of my longing
mixing the smell of cadavers with the scent of cinnamon tea

Nowadays, fish here
don't swim in water
the sound of guns has the might to mutate

n aprann respire tèt anba
San nou bat kou bal pingpong
nan fè nwa

Kwè m si ou vle
ma pa ka di ki jan m renmen w
Lè lanmou vle fè demitou
sou Granri
solèy pa nou
chavire grenn maldyòk
Li kontrarye lannuit

16

Lè lespri m bouke chache limyè
nan kwen miray
mwen kite w rakonte istaw n
sòti depi zantray lanmè
rive nan lonbraj dan w sou pwent cheve m

Nan ki lang pou m pale avè w
lè m anvi mòde w
jis yon gou latè fann nou an de
Se pa pou nou lalin ka bèl
si limyè nan je w
pa ka mare lakansyèl

we learn to breath upside down
Our blood beats like ping-pong balls
in the dark

Believe me
I can't say how I love you
When love wants to make a u-turn
on Grand Rue
our own sun
overturning cursed seeds
Upsetting the night

16

When my mind grows tired of seeking light
in corners
I let you tell our story
that comes from the belly of the sea
and reaches the shadow of your teeth at the tips of my hair

In what language should I speak to you
when I want to bite you
until the taste of the earth splits us in two
The moon isn't beautiful for us
if the light of your eyes
can't bind the rainbow

17

Poutan
lavi gen jou li di *je t'aime*
Jou sa yo de bra w fè lavironn kè m
figi w benyen nan fon je m
ou vlope m pa andedan san nou pa bezwen chanje po

Nan ki lang pou m pale avè w
lè vwa w pa bezwen louvri
pou mwen reponn antre cheri
Toutrèl depoze yon dènye kras lanmou
sou pwent bouch nou
pou n fè lawout

18

Mwen chache adrès ou sou entènet
Ou se sèl papiyon sou pye lorye
yon gato lèwa ki pa bezwen payèt
non w danse solo san l pa glise

Pa mande m ki lane nou te kontre
Kalandriye m chire an mil mòsò
Nan ki lang pou m pale avè w
lè m anvi ri
anvan almanak mande m konte plis paj

17

Yet
Life has days in which it says *je t'aime*
On those days your arms surround my heart
Your face bathes in the depths of my eyes
You wrap me from inside, we don't need to change skins

In what language should I speak to you
when you don't need to speak
for me to answer enter sweetheart
Doves drop a final bit of love
on the edge of our mouths
for the road

18

I look for your address on the internet
You are the laurel tree's only butterfly
A King's Day cake that needs no sprinkles
your name dances solo without slipping

Don't ask me what year we met
My calendar's torn in a million pieces
In which language should I speak to you
when I want to laugh
before the calendar asks me to count more pages

19

M plonje nan zile w san m pa konn naje
avèk soulye granmoun mwen
mare nan ren m

Ou louvri bouch pou ou nonmen non m
plidetwal krisifye lespas

20

Anba poto elektrik nan on bak machann
je m tonbe sou po w
kou dantèl blan sou soulye vèni
Nan ki lang pou m pale avè w
lè bri kè nou pentire kat kwen on peyi

Je fèmen nou fè lanmou
Mwen travèse rèv ou
sòti Savanèt rive Manich
Ke rad nou mare nan on pye flanbwayan
toupre Plezans

21

Pa mande m pouki bouch mwen tranble
lè lodè bonè karese lespri m
Syèl la tankou lekòl lage
Timoun sanzinifòm sote kòd ak loraj

M pa p konn kote pou m kache
si vwa a pase sou po m san l pa rete

19

I plunge into your island not knowing how to swim
with my grown-up shoes
tied to my hips

You open your mouth to speak my name
a rain of stars crucifies the space

20

Beneath the lightpost by a vendor's display case
my eyes fell upon your skin
like white lace on polished shoes
In what language should I speak to you
when the sound of our hearts
paints the four corners of a country

We make love eyes closed
I cross your dreams
from Savanèt all the way to Manich
The tails of our clothes are tied to flamboyant trees
near Plaisance

21

Don't ask me why my mouth trembles
when the scent of happiness strokes my mind
The sky strikes the school's closing bell
kids freed of uniforms skip rope with thunder

I won't know where to hide
if your voice brushes over my skin without stopping

22

Plezi a pran m pasipriz
Li teke m
tankou timoso lalin li glise sou po m
yon zetwal filant karese memwa m
tout kote li te ajenou
ap tann
san l pa t konnen
ki lè plezi a t ap tounen
pran m
pasipriz
sanzatann

23

Jodi a kè m rekonèt sa k pou li
li tranble kou fèy papye anba pwent kreyon
Mwen ranmase plezi a anvan l vole
tankou yon balon wouj
lè van karèm ap soufle

Mwen te renmen w ayè
epòk tipwentikwa te anvayi lespri m
mwen renmen w granm maten
lè rèv nou pale menm lang
m anvi renmen w demen
jis nou klere zantray lanmè

22

The pleasure took me by surprise
It tapped me like a marble
like a sliver of moon it slid onto my skin
a shooting star caressing my memory
in all the places it had been on its knees
waiting
not knowing
when the pleasure would return
to take me
by surprise
suddenly

23

Today, my heart recognizes what belongs to it
It trembles like a sheet of paper beneath a pencil tip
I gather up the pleasure before it flies off
like a red balloon
in the Lenten winds

I loved you yesterday
in the time of children's games
I love you in early morning
when our dreams speak the same language
I want to love you tomorrow
to the point of lighting the depths of the sea

24

menm lè m bliye koulè cheve w
lanmou m toujou pòtre avè w

Ou antre anba po m
kou plidetwal nan mitan lannuit

25

Pa mande m ki wout mwen fè
Lanmè pase lang li sou pye m
Pou m pa pèdi nan mitan mistè ak deblozay latè

M kanpe devan pòt ou
bra m chaje
kè m leje
Se ou ka di m sa pou m kite
Men m deja konnen m ap debake

Mwen sèmante lavi ka bèl

29
Peyi m

Gen kote lannuit tabli devan pòt kay
menm lè solèy leve
Gen kote timoun dòmi dèyè do nyaj
          pou yo pa tande san koule
Fanm bliye pote pitit
Gason zipe bouch yo jis nan je
Gen kote lavi bay payèt

24

Even when I forget your hair's color
My love resembles you

You've gotten under my skin
like a rain of stars at night

25

Don't ask me which way I go
The sea licks my feet
So I'm not lost in the mystery and turmoil of the earth

Here I am at your door
Arms full
Heart light
It's you who should tell me what to leave behind
Since I already know I'm coming

I swear that life can be beautiful

29
My Country

There are places where night sits at the front door
even at sunrise
There are places where children sleep behind clouds
          so they won't hear blood being shed
Where women forget to bear children
Where men zip their lips up to their eyes
There are places where life doles out sparkles

machin ponn lajan ak entènèt
   pou mistifye fènwa
Lannuit klere kou rad tafta premye janvye
   nan tan lontan
   avan pèpè
   anvan jennfi mouri nan ti pyès kay
   nan RiTimas
Gen kote limyè pa bezwen fil elektrik
Li gaye sèvèl timoun fronte
san l pa di tanpri souple

30
Epi gen peyi laj pa konte
timoun mete pye sou tèt granmoun
pou yo tete zetwal
lavi a bat san l pa fè m mal
Se yon peyi
kote m ale lè m anvi sou
Li bèl kou premye jou nou te kontre
li dous, li peze nan memwa m
li lejè tankou vwal sou do lanmè
Li laj kou paj liv van an ta pote
li di m mèvèy latè
ak tout sekrè lanmou
anvan m te poze je sou ou

La, lanmè kite plas
pou l ranmase tout anvi kriye m
Se yon peyi
kote m ale lè m anvi renmen jis mwen fou

cash machines and the internet
      to confuse the dark
Where night is as lit up as a taffeta dress on January first
      in the old days
        before second-hand clothes
        before girls died in forgotten rooms
      on Rue Tiremasse
There are places where light doesn't need electric wires
travelling permit-free
across the minds of rebellious children

30

There is a country where age does not matter
where children climb atop the heads of adults
to drink the strong milk of the stars
where life churns without hurting me
It's a country
I visit when I want to be drunk
It's as beautiful as the day we met
It's sweet, full in my memory
It's as light as a sail on the back of the sea
It's as wide as the page of the book the wind carries away
It speaks to me of the wonders of the world
and all the secrets of love
before I laid eyes on you

There, the sea makes a space
in which to gather all my tears
It is a country
where I go when I wish to love madly

31

Mwen di

Pou Ana

Yon ti bout moun antre nan fon memwa m
Li di pouki lapli kite mak sou lanmè
Pouki lèzòm derefize vole ba
lè zetwal ap file

Mwen di:
Se te yon fwa
Yon peyi tèt chòv ki batize nan afè pa bon
Li ekri nom m twa fwa
tankou yon chante manman m dòmi
kite pou mwen san l pa mouri

32

Se te yon fwa
Yon lang ki fè pye m leje
Li pase plim poul sou tout anvi m
Li ban m lespri doubout
tankou tizweso
          sou kab elektrik
zèl yo pa regade pèsonn
van sèl konnen ki lè yo ka vole

31

I Said

for Ana

A tiny bit of a girl entered the depths of my memory
asking why the rain leaves its marks on the sea
Why people refuse to fly low
When stars shoot across the sky

I said:
There was once
A bald-headed country baptized in need
It wrote my name three times
like a song my mother dreamed of
and left for me without even dying

32

There was once
A tongue that made my feet light
That tickled all my desires
That gave me a rebel spirit
like the birds
         on the electric wires
whose wings are not your business
only the wind knows when they might fly off

33

Yon tifi je kale bezwen pase
li mande kote pou m fè
wout ak baryè sa k pi laj?
wout ak pasdlo sa k pi long?

Yon ti bebe fronte mande wout pou l pase
kote l prale?

Mwen di
Se te yon fwa
yon peyi
Tèt li rete anba bra l
Epoutan
kouray li grenpe tèt mòn
bèlte l mare syèl ak lanmè
kote lavi pap janm mouri
Non l chita sou pwent lang mwen
tankou yon chante ki twò bèl pou l fini

34

M kase pla men m an de
pou m ranmase plis zetwal
paske
yon tibebe ki bezwen mache
mande m wout pou l pase

Sòti Tounapouna rive Laskaobas
Janbe Nouyòksiti ateri PòMago
Travèse movezè
sanble retay loraj
pou listwa sispann bliye

33

A clear-eyed girl seeks passage
She asks *which path should I take?*
What is wider, the road or the gate?
Which is longer, the road or the ford?

A boisterous child seeks passage
where is she going?

I say
There was once
a country
With its head buried in its arms
Yet with
Strength that reached mountain tops
with beauty that bound its sky and sea
where life will never die
Its name sits on the tip of my tongue
like a song too beautiful to end

34

I uncrease my hand
to collect more stars
because
a child wanting to walk
has asked me for passage

From Tunapuna to Lascahobas
Over to New York City landing in Port-Margot
Past the evil eyes
gathering the remnants of thunder
so history stops forgetting

Se yon peyi tètanba
De bra l louvri
nan chak liv mwen li
Lanmou l pa pran presyon
Nan pla men m se ladènyè kirestera

Se yon tifi je kale
de bra l louvri
depi jou li di lavi bonjou
nan yon ti peyi
kote nou tou de ap aprann grandi

35
Pou 2004

Ki peyi n ap kite dèyè?

Nan ki peyi nou ye si timoun ka mouri
pase manman yo pran bal nan tèt
san zòt pa sezi?
Ki peyi nap kite dèyè si timoun sispann rele
anvan yo pran premye tete?

Premye janvye rive yon jou twò ta
Sonnen tenèb pou bare wout lougawou
anvan l fè nwa

Lavi twò bel pou timoun kontinye mouri
san men yo pa janm karese zetwal
Mwen di twòp timoun mouri
Pase zòt jwe mab ak lavi

It's a country overturned
With arms outstretched
in every book I've read
Its love does not bend under pressure
In the palm of my hand it's the last one standing

It's a clear-eyed girl
with arms outstretched
since the day she greeted life
in a small country
where we are both learning to grow

35
For 2004

What country are we leaving behind?

In which country are we living if children can die
because their mothers are shot in the head
with no one being shocked
What country are we leaving behind if children stop crying
before their first breast?

January first comes a day too late
Sound the knell to bar the werewolves
before dark

Life is too beautiful for children to keep dying
before their hands have caressed stars
I say too many children die
Because others play with life

mache sou li
pile l
prije l jis san pete nan tout pas dlo
sou wout Grandans

36
Mwen di twòp timoun mouri
Anvan peyi dAyiti granmoun tèt li
ak tout papye l siyen an de kopi
Youn pou achiv
Youn pou l remèt yon tibebe ki vle grandi
San pèsonn detounen lespwa
nan lakou lopital jeneral

37
Ki peyi n ap kite dèyè?
Ki 2004 n ap fete lè bal ap jwe lago ak zantray
timoun nan Gonayiv?

Ak ki moun n ap fè lawout
Si nou bije charye bebe nan bwat
Si tete manman setoblije fèmen anvan laj?

Mwen di twòp timoun mouri

Lavi ka bèl
Lavi twò bèl
Pou n pa batay wete tout vye dèt
plis ipotèk zòt met sou dèt

walk on it
stomp on it
squeeze it until blood gushes from all the fords
on the road to Grand'Anse

36
I say too many children die
Before Haiti rules itself
With all its papers signed in duplicate
A copy for the archives
A copy for the baby who wants to grow
With no rerouting of hope
on the General Hospital grounds

37
What country are we leaving behind?
What 2004 will we celebrate when bullets play tag with children's
guts in Gonaïves?

Who will we walk beside
If we have to cart babies in boxes
If a mother's milk dries up too soon?

I say too many children die

Life can be beautiful
Life is too beautiful
For us not to fight against all the old debts
And the mortgages on those debts

Pou timoun sispann pè jwe ak lonbraj
Pou timoun aprann jwe ak loraj
Jis nou rive manyen zetwal

38
Ala dlo mwen ta seche

Pou tout timoun Gonayiv

Li pran m nan kè
tankou yon tranche ki pèdi wout
Li pran m nan tèt
tankou yon lwa ki pèdi memwa l

Doulè sa a se nan on sèl lang li ka rele

pa mande l bo w debò
pa mande l danse kole

Li pran m nan pwent pye m
m pliye ande
tèt anba
brazankwa

Si m te ka redefini listwa
ala paj m ta efase
Si m te ka pentire listwa
ala dlo mwen ta seche

Doulè sa a se yon sèl lang li ka pale

For children to not fear shadows
For children to learn to play with thunder
For us to touch the stars

38
What Water Wouldn't I Dry

for the children of Gonaïves

It gripped my heart
like a lost pang of childbirth
It gripped my head
like a *lwa* that lost its memory

This pain can only yell in one language

don't ask it to kiss you on both cheeks
don't ask it to slow dance

It invaded my feet
It bent me in two
upside down
cross armed

If I could rewrite history
I would erase so many pages
If I could paint history
what water wouldn't I dry

This pain can only speak one language

39
Zanmi

Lè figi m make laj mwen
lè m bouke souri pou zòt pa gade m nan je
lè m anvi di lavi bliye non m
kite m defigire chagren m
       janm vle
       angwo ou andetay
jou kègrenn kenbe m anba vant
Lè doulè a pliye m an plizyè moso
San m pa bije benyen
zanmi, ou pase santi bon sou mwen
Ou ranmase m ak tout rad sal

Lè lavi ban m anvi chante
Menm si je w plen dlo
zanmi, ou pa meprize kè kontan m
ou voye chagren w soukote
Ou ranmase m ak tout bonè m

Lè non w vin danse nan lespri m
san l pa prese
san l pa jennen pèsonn
Zanmi, yon seri koulè pi bèl

39
Friend

When my face shows my age
when I'm tired of smiling, so no one looks me in the eye
when I want to say to life *forget my name*
let me mar my grief
> *the way I want to*
> *in great or small gestures*

when days of grief keep me down
When the pain folds me into pieces
friend, you pick me up in my dirty clothes
You make me clean, you perfume me

When life gives me the urge to sing
Even if your eyes are full of tears
friend, you don't despise my happiness
you throw your grief aside
You pick me up in all my joy

When your name comes dancing in my mind
without hurrying
without bothering anyone
Friend, colors more beautiful

40
pase tanpase nan bouch granmoun
pi bèl pase lespwa nan men tibebe
mache anndan m

Ou ban m zèl pou m mòde lavi jis li tranble

40

than the long-ago times in the mouths of elders
more beautiful than hope in the hands of infants
walk inside me

You give me wings and let me bite life until it quivers

MARIE-CÉLIE AGNANT

Balafres | Gashes

Euménides

J'ai dans le corps des manières
de torrents en délire
grondements de terre en soubresauts
rebelle

La révolte dans le corps
ancrée
dès la première aube

dans la langue des hommes
point de mots
pour peindre mes remous

J'ai dans le corps des mots fous
déferlent
cendres soufre laves

et le temps depuis les Érinyes
dans mon corps
n'est plus temps

soifs
montagnes
roches chauffées à blanc
éclats

Euménides

My body holds the habits
of delirious torrents
of rumblings of earth
in rebellious jolts

revolt in the body
fixed
since the first dawn

humanity's tongues
have no words
for my whirlwinds

my body holds wild
words surging
sulfur ashes lava

and time since the Érinyes
in my body
is no more

thirst
mountains
stones heated white
shards

Incandescences

Dans les couloirs de ma mémoire
trimbale
ce ballot de souvenirs cassés
daïva
receleur
tour à tour
au gré des jours
un homme affamé
se mue en taureau
hanches en cadence
au rythme de la rage
pieds confondus avec l'asphalte
souvenirs
relents de tafia
de mangues pourries
marchands de bouteilles
babioles
fatras
Marias édentées croulant sous la crasse
cour des miracles
rigoles de fiente
berceau d'enfants nègres
friture rancie
recuite
au soleil
et cet écho de mouches
d'abeilles
rires acides
bonbon sirop
gingembrette

Incandescences

In the corridors of my memory
in the bundle of broken keepsakes
roams
daïva
hustler
depending on the day
a man so hungry
he becomes a bull
hips lifting and falling
to the rhythm of rage
feet merging with asphalt
memories
the smell of liquor
rotten mangoes
sellers of bottles
trinkets
stuff
toothless Marias crumbling under filth
courtyard of miracles
shit-drains
cradle of black children
rancid fried food
refried
in the sun
and this echo of flies
of bees
of acid laughter
bonbon sirop
gingerbread

l'égout hurle sa puanteur
dans les couloirs de ma mémoire
les souvenirs
abrupts
désespérances
inconfortables
vertiges
cortège de momies
symphonie d'angoisses
baignés de sueurs
et de boues

sewer spitting up its stench
in the corridors of my memory
abrupt recollections
desperate
prickly
dizzying
procession of mummies
symphony of anxieties
sweatbaths
and mud

Balafre

Sur les rides du monde
pour conjurer l'oubli
je veux écrire

un long poème

Les ongles plantés dans l'écorce de la terre
au creux du mensonge
je veux écrire

des phrases-témoins

Sur tous les silences complices
je veux ma plume

Torrent cavalcade
je veux ma plume

Ciseau
je veux ma plume

Et réinventer ta vérité

Ô Monde

Gash

On the world's wrinkles
to fend off forgetfulness
I want to write

a long poem

Fingernails planted in the peel of the earth
deep in the lie
I want to write

phrases-of-witness

On all the complicit silences
I want my pen

Gush and procession
I want my pen

Chisel
I want my pen

Reinventing your truth

O World

Fête des mères

T'imaginer
en ce dimanche absent
absente ta vie
la musique
le parfum du poulet
les flageolets sauce
cadence les fourchettes
les voix familières

Tu repousses l'assiette
morte ta faim
et la tentation de changer ce défunt jour
en une mascarade

La pluie tombe et noie tes rêves
mille fois morts sur un paquet de lettres
et de photos jaunies

T'imaginer
en ce dimanche absent
ce dimanche c'est novembre
novembre au mois de mai

En quête de réponses
pour continuer à vivre
tu veilleras
aussi longtemps
que tes larmes

Mother's Day

To imagine yourself
gone this Sunday
gone from your life
the music
the scent of chicken
bean sauce
cadence of forks
the familiar voices

Your hunger dead
you push back your plate
push back the urge to trick
this useless day

The rain falls drowning your dreams
a thousand times spent on a packet of letters
on faded photographs

To imagine yourself
gone this Sunday
Sunday in November
November in the month of May

With the wish for a way
to go on
you will watch
as long
as your tears fall

Imaginer
tes faims obstinées
sous les éternités grises
mère-taupe-femme-fille
tel cet indigent
à l'hospice
ton existence hoquète
abandonnée

Trois heures trente du matin
tu ne vas pas à la mosquée il y a du sable sous tes pas
et le désert

Tu vas à l'église inventer une prière
comme un cri

Tu vas à l'église
inventer un rêve
pour un dimanche absent

Sainte Marie Mère de Dieu priez pour lui
t'imaginer en ce dimanche
objet au pied d'un autel

To imagine
your headstrong hungers
beneath a grey eternity
mother-mole-woman-girl
like this pauper
at the hospice
your life hiccups
it gives up

Three thirty a.m.
you don't go to the mosque
there is sand beneath your feet
there is the desert

You go to church to invent
a prayer like a shout

You go to church
to invent a dream
for a Sunday gone

Holy Mary Mother of God pray for him
to see yourself this Sunday
at an altar's foot

Invitation

Dans le secret d'un simple bonheur
je te donne rendez-vous

là-bas

Il y aura ce jour-là
tout comme avant
des coqs qui chantent le matin mouillé
des hommes qui se lèvent
durs et forts
pour embrasser les champs
des femmes qui sèment
le printemps
égrennent la vie

Je te donne rendez-vous
dans ce vêtement de désir
mystère d'éternité sans cesse
renouvelé,
je t'attendrai

Il y aura ce jour-là
tout comme avant
des enfants
sourires de lune en goguette
heureux
comme promesses d'amour

Je te donne rendez-vous
laisse ici
infortunes narquoises

Invitation

In the secret of a simple joy
I set a time with you

over there

The day will be
as before
roosters crowing the morning wet
men rising
solid and strong
to wrap their arms around the fields
women sowing
springtime
planting life's seeds

I set a time with you
in a dress of desire
eternity's mystery unending
renewed
I will wait for you

On that day,
children
as before,
their moonlit smiles
happy
as love's promises

I set a time with you
let us set down
sly misfortune

débris d'incertitudes
je te donne rendez-vous
pour renaître
avec toi
sur les ailes d'une vague
retrouver nos visages oubliés
au hasard des sillons de cette terre

Assoiffés de tous les chemins de l'existence,
nous boirons la mer et
dans ce secret d'un bonheur simple
nous mourons
la vie
notre âme
notre île
dans la poitrine un cri d'innocence
ta vie
égarée dans la mienne

set down
the debris of doubt
I set a time with you
to be reborn
with you
on the wings of a wave
to re-find our faces
buried in the furrows of this earth

Thirsty for all the ways to be
we drink the sea and
in this secret of a simple joy
we die
life
our soul
our island
in the chest a shout of innocence
your life
lost in mine

Maëlstrom

Laisse-moi je t'en prie
comme on va à l'école
le temps
d'apprendre l'amour
mais à tue-tête quand brûle la fièvre
mon corps
sans rancune et sans souvenance
flamme dans la tempête
s'affole
tout est inutile
sauf du frémissement
le sublime
et de l'instant . . .
la dernière perle

Maelstrom

Give me, please,
as if going to class
the time
to learn love
but out loud when fever burns
my body
free of hard feelings free of recollection
flame in the storm
maddening
all things useless
but the trembling
the sublime
and the moment . . .
the last pearl

Deuxième cri

Sarabande d'étoiles fécondes
sceptre à la main
le jour avait éclos

puis le soir impie
rafales d'illusions

du banquet
il ne reste que trognons et rognures
pour des rois devenus ilotes

ce n'est rien . . .
le destin s'est trompé

Second Shout

Saraband of fertile stars
scepter in hand
the day unfurls

then the irreverent night
gusts of illusions

of the feast
only cores and trimmings
remain for kings become slaves

it's nothing . . .
fate had it wrong

Troisième cri

La parole a fui au loin
seul demeure le cri
et chaque nuit
sur le pas de nos portes
abandonne
sa brassée de chimères

Third Shout

The word has fled
what remains is the shout
and every night
on our thresholds
its armful of chimera

Dernier cri

Au galop la colère
prend d'assaut les vestiges des consciences
poursuivons ces mains sacrilèges
qui à pleines dents
effeuillent l'existence
plumes au vent
grises ou blanches
plumes sans but
noires ou jaunes
plumes sans port
âmes errantes . . .

Last Shout

Galloping anger storms
what's left of the conscience
chase then those unholy hands
fully-teethed
that pluck existence
that hurl feathers to the wind
grey or white
aimless feathers
black or yellow
feathers with no roosts
souls adrift . . .

Nocturne

Telle une biche effrayée
j'ai vu le jour
la vie m'a traversée
vierge folle
et j'ai donné naissance à des hommes
au regard balayé
par des vents d'errance et de peur
qui veillera mon espérance?

Nocturne

I was born
like a frightened doe
life crossed me
mad virgin
I gave birth to men
with gazes swept
by the winds of fear and wandering
who will watch over my hope?

Brasero

À la mémoire de Gérald Brisson

Tu es parti
tu as laissé cette maison
englouti par la solitude
et ce journal
inachevé

sur la table
une lampe
ne veut pas mourir
des papillons imprudents
à l'entour

la clé est sur la porte
les ronces ont envahi le porche
les oiseaux sont partis
les voisins se signent:
prestement . . . ils passent . . . tu es parti
mais l'empreinte de ton sourire
indélébile
sur le visage du matin assiégé
l'écho de ta voix nous talonne
brûlant

Tu es parti
Tu as laissé ton cœur BRASERO
dans le ventre de l'île
ton sang goutte à goutte
dans ses veines
s'est infiltré
la clé est sur la porte
la lampe luit encore

Brasero

in memory of Gérald Brisson

You have gone
you have left this house
engulfed in loneliness
this journal
unfinished

on the table
a lamp
unwilling to die
reckless butterflies
around it

the key is in the lock
the brambles have overtaken the porch
the birds are gone
the neighbors make the sign of the cross
quickly . . . they pass . . . you have gone
but the stamp of your smile
remains
on the besieged face of morning
the echo of your voice burning
on our heels

You have gone
leaving your heart BRASERO
in the island's belly
your blood drop by drop
entering
its veins
the key in the lock
the lamp still shining

Blues pour l'Azanie

Sur Roben Island un arbre a poussé
nourri à la sève Xhosa
ses racines ont laissé des sentiers d'espoir
à la mémoire de tes ghettos Ô Azanie
Madiba, Madiba
les branches
d'un bantoustan à l'autre s'étendent
Madiba
écoute Madiba
les tambours Xhosas
empruntent tes sentiers

Dans la grisaille d'Orange
une reine va
elle chante Madiba
mon pays, mon amour
sa voix est un serpent qui étrangle Brandfort la blanche
banissez-la
exilez-la
les tambours Xhosa retrouveront ses pas

Sur les barbelés de Soweto
des larmes sont restées figées
abasourdies
récifs en colère jaillis des prunelles lourdes de vos enfants

Zamie, Madiba
l'Azanie est un blues immense
dans la nuit noire
comme un long fleuve en rut
vos enfants aux prunelles lourdes
chevauchent des tambours Xhosas

Blues for Azania

On Roben Island a tree grew
fed by Xhosa sap
roots bequeathing ways of hope
remembering your ghettos O Azania
Madiba, Madiba
the branches
of one bantustan extend to another
Madiba
hear Madiba
how the Xhosa drums
follow you

In the gray of Orange
a queen walks
she sings Madiba
my country, my love
her voice is a snake that strangles white Brandfort
banish her
exile her
the Xhosa drums will find their way again

On Soweto's barbed wire
tears linger frozen
stunned
enraged reefs sprung from the heavy eyes of your children

Zamie, Madiba
the Azania is a massive blues
in the black night
like a long river on fire
your children with heavy eyes
riding Xhosa drums

Manuel

Il a vu le jour dans la grisaille et le mépris
dans les narines le souffle sauvage
des tambours écorchés

Il a senti la nuit
nuit après nuit
s'étaler sur ses faims

Il a vu les aubes innocentes
danser sur les collines
coutelas au poing

Il a poussé
herbe drue
le front lourd des sarcasmes des nantis
ailes déployées
sur les berges des torrents que l'on croyait
domptés

Il a passé des nuits vaines
vaines nuits
à calfeutrer l'espérance et

son regard d'hélianthe
s'est inscrit
dans les replis du jour

Il a poussé herbe drue
la sève rougie
le rictus au bord de l'œil

Manuel

He was born in greyness and disdain
wild breath of flayed drums
in his nostrils

He felt the night,
night after night,
spread over his hunger

He saw innocent dawns
dance on the hills
cutlass in hand

He grew
like thick grass
brow bearing the scorn of the rich
wings spread
on the banks of torrents thought
tamed

He spent useless nights
pointless nights
rainproofing hope

with a gaze bright as a sunflower
written
into the folds of the day

He grew like thick grass
with its reddened sap
clear-eyed

coriace
les racines cagneuses
suffocant dans la fange

la fange foisonne
fourmille
enfle
éclate
éclabousse
sans fard
sans fausse sagesse

strong
his knock-kneed roots
suffocating in the mire

and the mire abounding
teeming
swelling
bursting
splashing
with no whitewash
with no false wisdom

La gésine

Elle venait de nulle part
Elle allait dans le pays gangrené
la chimère collée à la peau
une cuirasse

Elle allait citant Lorca
la voix éclatée tel un fleuve emporté
les poings levés

il se disait qu'elle s'était enfuie
de l'asile
on ne sait
qu'elle était maudite

Quand sa voix enveloppait le vent
les mères sous leurs jupons cachaient les enfants

Elle disait *regardez-moi, je suis grosse*
depuis des lunes
j'attends que mes époux reviennent
et je mettrai au monde un ouragan
pour faire bondir de la cendre des chiens endormis

Certains soirs on l'entendait chanter
ses mots parcouraient les déserts arides
les villes catacombes
sa voix lacérait le vent
mettait le prurit aux mémoires
regardez-moi
dans mon ventre enflammé je porte les rêves des hommes

La Gésine

She came from nowhere
She went about the gangrenous country
impossible fantasies stuck to the skin
like armor

She went quoting Lorca
voice bursting like a run-away river
fists raised

They say she fled
the asylum
we don't know
if she was cursed

When her voice held the wind
mothers hid their children in their skirts

She said *look at me, I've been pregnant*
for so long
waiting for my husbands to return
so I can deliver a hurricane
so I can make sleeping dogs leap from the ashes

Certain nights we heard Her singing
words crossing dry deserts
cities of catacombs
voice shredding the wind
making memories itch
look at me
I bear the dreams of men in my swollen belly

ils sont semé dans mon jardin des braises de liberté
dans mes reins je berce la fougue des hommes

et le pays affolé frissonnait lorsqu'Elle écrivait
sur les ailes du vent
les noms de ses hommes . . .

Elle venait de nulle part
Elle disait chanter pour passer le temps
attendre que ses hommes reviennent

son chant montait
enflait l'océan
crevait l'horizon
J'entends passer le souffle du diable
les feuilles des arbres tombent tombent sans trêve
courent se réfugier derrière les portes des
grand-mères
les grands-mères percluses qui ne balaient plus
qui ne se bercent plus sur le pas des portes
avec les grimaces sous les paupières
elles tremblent
et poussent les volets
elles entendent passer le souffle du diable

Son chant décoiffait les maisons
pénétrait sous les lits
les couilles des chiens endormis
claquaient des dents
J'entends passer le souffle du diable
les roseaux ne danseront plus du rythme des battoirs des femmes
les femmes sont parties les mains sèches
les seins vides

The coals of freedom set in my garden
I cradle the passions of men in my loins

and the panicked country shivered when She wrote
on the wings of the wind
the names of her men . . .

She came from nowhere
She sang to pass the time
waiting for her men to return

Her song rose
took over the ocean
split the horizon open
I hear the devil's breath blow by
the leaves of the trees fall, fall without stopping
scurrying to hide behind grandmothers' doors
crippled grandmothers who no longer sweep
who don't rock themselves on doorsteps
with scowls under their eyelids
they tremble
and close the shutters tight
they hear the devil's breath blow by

Her song rocked the houses
slid under the beds
entered the testicles of sleeping dogs
made teeth chatter
I hear the devil's breath blow by
the reeds won't dance again in time with the washboards
the women left with dry hands
with empty breasts

elles sont parties
l'Aube s'est fourvoyée

Son chant montait obstiné
si mes paroles ont goût d'amertume
c'est que ma rage tremble
les vautours sont lâchés
éclaboussent le jour
j'étouffe!
ce pays gangrené
trop petit pour ma haine
ma voix est un surin
ma voix est un stylet
que dis-je?
rafale de venin qui s'impatiente sur l'abîme
ma voix siffle exaspérée
puisque les chiens se taisent . . .

Si mes paroles ont goût d'amertume
dans ce pays les hommes ne sont plus des hommes
ils marchent de biais
les crocs dehors
le cul béant
vendent leur mère et leurs filles
vitriolent les rêves des enfants

Si mes paroles ont goût d'amertume
il y a tout ce sang
ce sang lourd
qui engrosse ma terre défigurée depuis tant de lunes Aie . . .
si j'ai si mal
je dégueule
je crache

they left
Dawn went astray

Her song rose stubbornly
if my words taste bitter
it's because my rage shakes
the vultures are let loose
to rip open the day
I'm choking
this gangrenous country
is too small for my hate
my voice is a dagger
my voice is a pen
what am I saying?
my voice hisses
spray of venom maddened by the void
because the dogs are silent . . .

If my words taste bitter
in this country, men are no longer men
they walk sideways
fangs out
asses wide open
selling their mothers and daughters
killing children's dreams

If my words have a bitter taste
there is all this blood
this heavy blood
soaking my scarred land for so long Aie . . .
if I suffer so much
if I yell
spit

me voilà dragon
serpent
je siffle
hurle
piaffe
c'est pour tous les chiens muets
tapis dans la cendre

Ma voix
ma vie
mes tripes
mes mots
pourquoi?
si je ne peux hurler au monde
que l'aube s'est fourvoyée

Je suis grosse depuis des lunes
j'attends que mes hommes reviennent
l'ouragan
de ma vie écartelée
bientôt jaillira
par tous les chemins muets.

become a snake
a dragon
hiss
howl
stomp
it's for all the mute dogs
buried in the ash

My voice
my life
my guts
my words
why?
if I can't scream to the world
that the dawn has gone astray

I have been pregnant for so long
waiting for my men to return
the hurricane
of my torn life
will soon blow through
all the mute paths.

Abîmes

Poésie ma légende
inlassablement ruminée

mon cri cravaché

douleur sans contours
que je m'entête à évoquer

remonte sans cesse des abîmes

Au fond de ma gorge
plainte crevée

mots en syncope

vagues folles
vont et viennent
sur des pages interminables

poésie ma légende
mon éternité

une bouée sur l'écume des mots

Abysses

Poetry my legend
always thought of

my flogged yell

the shapeless pain
I insist on calling up

rising constantly from the void

Deep in my throat
the flat complaint

words in syncopation

mad waves
coming and going
on endless pages

poetry my legend
my eternity

a buoy on the foam of words

Mimose

J'avais une amie
une sœur
une compagne
on s'était rencontrées sans témoins

Nous lisions toutes les deux Victor Hugo
les Misérables
et nous pleurions
mêlant nos larmes
façonnant nos chagrins
en matins de vendanges

J'avais une amie
sur nos cahiers d'écolières les mêmes ratures
sur les pages de nos vies
les mêmes coups de griffes

Elle était comme moi de celle dont l'enfance
avait ce goût aigre des refus
de celles que les bourrasques
avaient trop ballotées

Les bourrasques m'ont traînée
sur les rives de l'exil
effiloché mes racines
des cheveux blancs et drus sur ma vie
ont germé
j'ai appris à parler avec d'autres mots

J'avais une camarade
parce que nos peines ne sont plus les mêmes

Mimose

I had
a sister
a partner
we met, unnoticed

We read Victor Hugo
Les Misérables
we cried
mixing our tears
shaping our sorrows
on mornings of bounty

I had a friend
we had the same scribbles in our school notebooks
on our life's pages we had
the same lines crossed out

She too came from people whose childhoods
tasted of sour refusal
people too buffeted
by the wind

The gusts dragged me
to exile's shores
frayed my roots
pushed thick white hair
onto my life
I learned to speak with new words

I had a friend
because our sorrows are no longer the same

parce que nous n'avons plus ces cahiers d'écolières
où s'inscrivent les mêmes rêves
parce qu'aujourd'hui
chacune un registre nous avons
énorme livre dur et sévère
ouvert pour chacune
sur un monde
séparé
distinct
inégal . . .

Je l'ai perdue
on ne se comprenait plus
je criais
elle balbutiait
j'allais les bras ouverts
pour étreindre la vie
la tête dans le ciel
elle allait
claquant des talons
bousculant tout ce que hier nous jetait dans l'émoi

J'ai perdu ma camarade
il me reste l'espoir
de ce printemps
où il faudra
sur la place publique juger
les fossoyeurs de notre enfance
parmi la foule
peut-être
elle sera là
on se tendra la main

because we don't have our school notebooks
in which we wrote the same dreams
because we each
have a different way now
a hard book stern and huge
open
onto worlds
separate
distinct
unequal . . .

I lost her
we no longer know each other
I shouted
she stammered
I went open-armed
to grab hold of life
head in the air
she went
heels clicking
shaking everything that had shaken us

I lost my comrade
what is left is hope
for the spring
that will let us
judge the gravediggers of our childhoods
in the public square
in the crowd
maybe
she'll be there
we'll reach out to one another

Sources Chaudes

Sources Chaudes
à l'ombre du manguier

Carmita rêve de vie

La mouche ronronne
passe
repasse

compte recompte ton existence
en compte-gouttes
Carmita tout en haillons

La mouche passe
repasse
frissonne
sous tes tropiques
Carmita

Égrenne tes mariages
sans robe blanche
sans couronne ni lune de miel

La mouche ronronne
passe
repasse
ton âme gronde
tel un orage
à Sources Chaudes

Sources Chaudes

In the shade of the Sources Chaudes
mango tree

Carmita dreams of life

A fly whirs
flies by
and by again

It mulls over your living
bit by bit
Carmita all in rags

The fly goes by
and by again
tremors
in your tropics
Carmita

Your weddings file by
with no white dresses
no crowns no honeymoons

The fly whirs
flies by
and by again
your soul rumbles
like a thunderstorm
at Sources Chaudes

Compte
recompte les épines
tous ces enfants
nés de sexes sans visages
sans histoires et sans noms

Aux halliers de la vie
tes haillons se déchirent
Carmita toute en lambeaux

tire l'aiguille
raccommode
ravaude la vie
Carmita

toute la vie
toute ta vie

It mulls over
once and again the thorns
the children
born of fathers with no faces
no histories no names

Your rags are torn
in life's thickets
Carmita in tatters

Draw the needle
mend
stitch together life
Carmita

all of life
all of life

Extase

À Cynthia
ma promesse de femme

Dors mon enfant
toute belle dans ton rêve
chandelle allumée
oiseau dans le ciel
vers la rive de ton choix

Trouve les cactus en fleurs
les clowns et les ballons
les parfums
la musique

Vole mon enfant
butine les oasis
les champs de lune

Goutte jusqu'aux miettes ton sommeil
Inscris dans ta mémoire
cette première extase

Dors mon enfant
c'est encore le printemps

Joy

To Cynthia
my promise of a woman

Sleep my child
so beautiful in your dream
burning candle
bird in the sky
toward the shore of your choosing

Find the cacti that flower
the clowns and balloons
the perfume
and music

Fly my child
forage the oases
the moon's fields

Taste your sleep to the last bit
stamp in your memory
this first joy

Sleep my child
it is still spring

Inventaire

Fleur Flamme Femme Fontaine
on t'a voulu vestale
on t'a voulu flamme
flamme-vestale femme-forteresse
pour veiller
conforter
donner vie
aux sexes fragiles
sexes frimas

On t'a voulu vestale-flamme-femme
femme-forteresse femme-nombril
femme d'estoc
fleur fragile
où s'engouffrent
les ondées éphémères des saisons de leurre

On t'a voulu rivière on t'a voulu crystal
fontaine-crystal
claire et muette rivière
troublante
généreuse d'ivresses
caverne d'Alibaba
on t'a voulu flamme-femme-fleur
crystal-fontaine
vestale-amazone
infibulée ouverte

On t'a voulu océan
ruisseau caverne

Inventory

Flower Flame Woman Fountain
they wanted you vestal
they wanted you flame
flame-vestal woman-fortress
to watch over
to comfort
to give life
to the fragility of men
to frost

They wanted you vestal-flame-woman
woman-fortress woman-navel
woman thrusting
delicate flower
engulfed by the transient waves
of attraction's seasons

They wanted you river they wanted you crystal
crystal-fountain
clear and mute river
troubling
giving intoxicating
cave of Alibaba
they wanted you flame-woman-flower
crystal-fountain
vestal-amazon
infibulated open

They wanted you ocean
cave stream

où se fourvoient
désirs confus
gauches et enchaînés
inassouvis
à jamais
muets et coupables

Femme sans bagages
sans souvenirs de ta part de rêve, tu vas
Trébuchant sur ta part de monde
tu vas
J'écris pour célébrer
ton corps d'indulgence
ébauché par mes lèvres si souvent maladroites
ton sexe affamé d'un souffle nouveau
dire
tes plus belles saisons
longtemps excisées

site of confused desires
gone astray
awkward chained
forever
wanting
mute guilty

Woman with no luggage
with no memories of your own dreams, you go
stumbling across your part of the world
you go
I write to celebrate
your body of indulgence
sketched by my often clumsy lips
your sex hungry for new breath
to express
your best seasons
long cut away

L'Étranger

Dans une trop grande ville
une ville triste et froide
seule
il y a un homme
seul
traîné par ses semelles fatiguées
sur les trottoirs
indifférents

Il ne va nulle part
personne ne l'attend

Dans ses poches
ses doigts caressent
des morceaux de papier
vieillis
reconnaissances inutiles
poussières d'espérances
mémoire calcinée de tant d'ailleurs défigurés

Cet homme
je le connais
je reconnais
les balafres de son cœur
dans les mêmes broussailles
nos vies se sont égarées

Cet homme est mon frère:
l'Étranger

The Stranger

In a too big city
in a sad and cold city
alone
a man
alone
dragged by his tired soles
along indifferent
sidewalks

Going nowhere
with no one waiting for him

In his pockets
his fingers
rub old pieces of paper
useless forms of I.D.
the dust of any hope
charred memories of so many disfigured elsewheres

I know
this man
I recognize
the scars of his heart
our lives gone astray
in the same underbrush

This man is my brother:
the Stranger

Nocturne II

Quand tu atteindras ce chemin
où tous les pas tous les visages
gauchement
se confondent

Tous les pas à moitié ivres
tous les visages le même regard
sur ce chemin où les années
comme une malédiction

Quand tu seras sur cette rive où
comme une épave la vie
au gré de ses tumultes
t'aura traîné

Et que tes jours et tes nuits
toutes heures enchevêtrées ne seront plus
qu'un seul et long hiver
avec ton âme
livrée à tous les vents

Emmène avec toi
ta tendresse et ta musique

Nocturne II

When you get to this place
where all paths and faces
ineptly
merge

The half-drunk steps
the faces all with the same look
on this road with its years
like a curse

When you reach this shore
like a wreck
with life through its tumults
having dragged you

When the tangled hours
of your days and your nights
are nothing
but a single long winter
and your soul
is handed over to the many winds

Take with you
your tenderness and your music

Orphée

Brise ta plume en vérité
je ne suis pas
cette nymphe exquise ni
cette madone emmurée
dans le grand livre de tes songes
Loin du royaume
des flonflons de tes mots
partons

Brise ta plume je ne suis pas
cette divine
cette fée
Aphrodite
aux yeux d'eau marine
qui hante tes rêves

Brise ta plume et ton miroir
regarde-moi et
aime moi
à pleines mains et
à plein corps

Aime ma peau
reflet des nuits de ton enfance
ma bouche
muscade frondeuse
mon corps
balafon d'obsidienne
mes cuisses bilimbao et
mon souffle touffeur de savane

Orpheus

Honestly, break your pen
I'm neither
exquisite nymph nor
Madonna walled
in the great book of your dreams
far from the realm and frippery
of your words
move on

Break your pen I am not
this goddess
fairy
Aphrodite
whose seawater eyes
haunt your dreams

Break your pen and your mirror
look at me and
love me
with both hands
full-bodied

Love my skin
dark as your childhood nights
my mouth
rebellious nutmeg
my body
obsidian balafon
my bilimbao thighs
the heat of my breath like a savannah's

Brise ta plume et ton miroir
égrenne ma chevelure
palma-cristi lianes sauvages
et tiens tes doigts loin de ta plume
ton cœur
hors de ces rêves
où dansent ces nymphes crystal aux regards d'eau d'azur
sous un ciel
bleu de nuages

Break your pen and your mirror
brush my hair
palma-christi wild lianas
and keep your fingers away from your pen
your heart
far from the dreams
in which crystal nymphs with their azure-water eyes dance
beneath a sky
blue with clouds

Vos grands pieds

Dix ans
Vingt ans
Trente ans
à genoux
vos grands pieds sur mon cou

Dix ans
Vingt ans
Trente ans
vos pieds de plomb
piaffent dansent la bacchanale
vos éperons me crucifient
me clouent au sol
je patauge dans mes sueurs

Dix ans
Vingt ans
Trente ans
vos grands pieds un jour
soudain gangrenés
tombent
comme un sexe vidé

Your Big Feet

Ten years
Twenty years
Thirty years
kneeling
your big feet on my neck

Ten years
Twenty years
Thirty years
your lead feet
stomping, dancing the bacchanal
spurs crucifying me
nailing me to the ground
I wade in my own sweat

Ten years
Twenty years
Thirty years
your big feet one day
suddenly gangrenous
falling
like an eviscerated sex

Vade mecum

Ne me racontez pas votre vie
je vous fais grâce de la mienne

nous irons ainsi à tâtons
mâchonnant nos incertitudes

avec nos rires estropiés
nos yeux criblés de mensonges

et nos vies
si mal baisées

ne me racontez pas votre vie
je ne vous dirai pas la mienne

côte à côte nous irons
sans nous voir sans nous toucher

et cet animal dans le ventre
la peur!

Ne me racontez pas votre vie!
sortons nos masques
nos défroques
nos fables
habillons-nous de rictus
de carnaval
de contre-vérités

Vade Mecum

Don't talk to me about your life
I'll spare you mine

we'll feel our way
chewing our uncertainties

with crippled laughter
eyes riddled with lies

our lives
so badly screwed

don't talk to me about your life
I won't bother you with mine

we'll go along side by side
not seeing not touching

and fear!
this animal in the belly

Don't talk to me about your life!
let's pull out our masks
our frocks
our stories
let's dress in carnival
grins
in fictions

Gardez bien au chaud tous vos secrets
je ne suis pas indiscrète
pas bavarde non plus

Je veux dire ces pays
d'interminables absences
dire aussi
que j'ai vu tant d'hommes
dévorés par la haine
attaqués par le fiel
telles les vagues voraces
sur la grève
ouvrant leurs gueules affamées

J'ai vu des étoiles se changer en larmes
lucioles égarées
je les ai vues

dégringoler du ciel
s'enfoncer à tout jamais
dans les entrailles de la terre

C'étaient des gosses
ils n'avaient pas vu
la rosée
ni ses promesses

Je ne veux pas vous importuner
mais avant que les sabots du silence ne couvrent ma voix

laissez-moi vous dire
que je suis née
la nuque

Keep all your secrets
I'm not indiscreet
not chatty either

I want to speak about those countries
of incessant absences
I want to say
I have seen so many men
swallowed by hate
attacked by gall
like the ravenous waves
on the shore
opening their hungry mouths

I have seen the stars change themselves into tears
lost fireflies
I have seen them

fall from the sky
and sink
into the earth's guts

like children
who never saw
the dew
or its promises

I won't bother you
but before the hooves of silence cover up my voice

let me tell you:
I was born
neck

entre le billot
et coutelas
ils m'ont dit *tu bouges*

À pas de loups j'ai semé mes geôliers mais là-bas
d'autres m'ont dit

si tu n'es pas content
retourne chez toi

Le désert s'allonge
pénible sous mes pas
je ne sais plus trouver le chemin de mon chez moi

mon chez moi en lambeaux
pièces dépareillées

Cette déchirure d'exil
tel un linceul s'étend sur ma vie
le temps me fait la nique
dans un long sanglot m'étreint

Avec les années
je ne suis même plus celle-ci
celle-là
celle d'à côté

Je suis devenue
la vague
à conjurer

la horde
à disperser

between the chopping block
and cutlass
they said *move*

I slipped past my jailers but past them
others said

go home
if you're not happy

The desert stretches on
burning my feet
I can't find my way home

my home is in tatters
scattered pieces

The tear of exile
is a shroud covering my life
time pisses me off
a long sob takes me over

Years go by
I am no longer that woman
that one
or the other one

I have become
the wave
to ward off

the horde
to dissolve

la houle
menaçante

j'arrive
je déferle

indécente

avec ma gueule de boula-boula

ma face de bougnoule

ma langue

mes coutumes

mon patrimoine

barbare

suspect

j'ai le culot de réclamer
du soleil
pour mes enfants

Ne m'écoutez plus si vous voulez
mais je dois crier
l'étau se resserre

jusqu'à laisser échapper la pourriture

L'étau se resserre

the swell
threatening

I arrive
I break

indecent

with my boula-boula mouth

my sand-nigger face

my tongue

my customs

my birthright

barbaric

shady

I have the nerve to ask
for some sun
for my children

Don't listen to me more than you want to
but I have to shout out
the vice tightens

until the rot escapes

The vice tightens

résonne depuis Sharpeville
cette mémoire

L'étau se resserre
retentissent les cris
cinq cents ans captifs

et parle Guacanagaric

et parle Anacaona
celle que l'on disait
fleur du Xaragua

L'étau se resserre
et crie les noms

de Tupac Amaru

de Caonabo

et parle Toussaint Louverture
au Fort de Joux
dans les montagnes du Jura

AINSI NAIT LA DOULEUR

celle-là même qui laboure nos rives
depuis les côtes d'Afrique

Ne me contez pas votre vie
mais moi je dois vous parler de tout ce qui fut mien

. . . ce qui fut mien

memory
ringing from Sharpeville

The vice tightens
on screams
five hundred years captive

And I hear Guacanagaric

I hear Anacaona
the one we called
flower of Xaragua

The vice tightens
shouting the names

Tupac Amaru

Caonabo

Toussaint Louverture
at Fort de Joux
in the Jura mountains

HERE IS HOW PAIN IS BORN

the very pain that plows our shores
from the African coasts

Don't talk to me about your life
but I have to speak about all that was mine

. . . that once was mine

Comme le souffle d'un pur-sang
ma voix se rue
Je ne veux pas du silence pour tromper ma blessure

même la nuque sur le billot
je ne mets pas d'eau dans mon vin
je m'enivre tous les jours
à la coupe du refus
et je vivrai mille existences
à Roben Island
avec la haine pour seule compagne

Je ne vous ai rien dit du tout

Et moi, je n'ai rien entendu

Mais dans cette vie à coups de hache
Dites . . .

Like the breath of a thoroughbred
my voice rushes
I won't let silence wrap my wound

even if my neck's on the block
I won't water down my wine
Every day
I drink from the cup of refusal
and live a thousand lives
on Roben Island with hate as my only companion

I've told you nothing at all

And me, I've heard nothing

But in this life of axe blows
Speak . . .

Jaculatoire

Estampille fidèle sur la mémoire
la campagne charriait des senteurs de canne brûlée
Souffle et caresse du vent sur mes paupières
Safran dans le pré
Pissenlits . . .
nul besoin de connaître votre nom
Fruits si doux et parfumés
Dons du ciel
qu'on égrène dans la bouche les baisers

Souvenirs
jeu de perles
de poussière
suspendues dans l'air tiède
Sous la table au crépuscule
en toute innocence
un chat dort et cligne des yeux

Mais dehors tout changeait
pour n'en laisser que le goût
comme après l'amour
ne subsistent que les contours
quand tout s'en va

Dans ma tête et dans mes veines cette musique
plaisir et tristesse
oracles du tambour
dévale la montagne

Fervent Prayer

Stamped in my memory, faithfully
the countryside bearing the scent of burnt cane
breath and caress of the wind on my eyelids
the meadow's saffron
dandelion . . .
no need to know your name
fruit so sweet and fragrant
gifts from heaven
whose kisses we peel into our mouths

Memories
string of pearls
of dust
dangling in the warm air
beneath the table at dusk
a cat sleeping innocently
eyes blinking

And outside everything changing
leaving only the taste
as after love
the contours
all else fading

In my head, in my veins, this music
pleasure and sadness
oracles of the drum
coming down the mountain

Cette musique sourde
porteuse dans l'échine
de si étranges frémissements
Mais déjà dehors
nuit de métal
le sang cascade dans les rigoles

This muffled music
carrying such strange quivers
down the spine
and already outside
the metal night
the blood cascading through the rills

Toi et moi

Légende et comédie le glas sonne
même les clowns sont si tristes
fard et silence emplissent la bouche
jusqu'à l'âme

Il ne reste crois-moi que
sur mon corps cette fête de ta bouche
de tes mains
en nous cette grenade qui éclate
à l'écoute des frissons

Évanouis
même les mirages
il ne reste crois-moi
que toi et moi
et le déluge sans nom qui l'envahit

You and Me

In legend or in comedy, the death-bell rings
even the clowns are so sad
blush and silence stuffing the mouth
up to the soul

Believe me, on my body
remains this feast of your mouth
of your hands
in us this grenade that explodes
at the sound of our shudders

With even the mirages
erased
you and I, believe me,
remain,
and the nameless deluge that claims us

Ma sœur

Contes de mousseline et d'organdi
elle rêvait d'un drap blanc
couronne d'étoiles sur ses seins
rubans et dentelles tremblantes
comme les feuilles sous la rosée
rubans et dentelles transparentes
à défaire goutte à goutte

Un homme aux yeux de légendes
pour lui conter les voyages qu'elle n'avait jamais faits
un homme aux mains comme des coquillages
pour lui dessiner de multiples paysages

Pour ses attentes frileuses
la légende a esquissé des venelles
où vont les fantômes

et une manière d'homme
les mains croisées dans le dos
une manière d'homme . . .
mort
le testament de la parole au fond des yeux

My Sister

Stories of muslin and organdy
she dreamt of white sheets
a crown of stars over her breasts
ribbons and lace trembling
like leaves beneath dew
translucent ribbons and lace
to be undone slowly

She dreamt of a man with great stories in his eyes
telling her of trips she had never taken
a man with hands as beautiful as shells
sketching for her the many landscapes

For her naïve hopes
Life's story drew alleys
where ghosts go

Life drew a type of man
with arms crossed behind his back
a type of man . . .
dead
the will of the word deep in his eyes

Il y avait

Il y avait la rue qui montait
tel un serpent lointain et sans âge
au bout de la rue la maison
les baies vitrées regorgeaient de soleil
bougainvillées et lauriers-roses
s'élançaient
à l'assaut des barricades
derrière les barricades il y avait Alice
Exilée de son corps
Alice n'avait connu ce pari de l'exubérance
Derrière les barricades vivait Alice
le grésillement prodigieux
d'un feu de brousse
sous les paupières
Il y avait la rue
qui ne reconnaissait pas
les pas d'Alice
elle allait de sa chambre
aux rideaux de dentelles
à la voiture qu'avançait
Oreste le garçon
Il y avait les rideaux
sans cesse tirés sur les baies
Alice et le tourbillon de son sang
Alice et ce désir sans prologue,
Alice incandescence,
les absences cruelles ravinaient son corps
Alice et la sueur qui par les nuits
de douce chaleur perlait
de son nombril prisonnier

There Was

There was the street rising
like a distant and ageless serpent
at the end of the street the house
bay windows full of sunlight
bougainvillea and oleander
rushing to
hurl themselves against the gates
behind the gates, Alice
exiled from her body
Alice not knowing this gamble of exuberance
behind the gates, Alice
of the immense crackling
bush fire
beneath the eyelids
there was the street
that knew nothing
of Alice's steps
from her room
with the lace curtains
to the car driven by
Oreste *the boy*
and the curtains
forever pulled across the bay windows
Alice and the whirlwind of her blood
Alice and this desire with no foreword
incandescent Alice
of cruel absences ravishing the body
Alice of the sweat on nights
of sweet warmth spilling
from her captive navel

Alice bout d'île sur une île
au bout de la rue
Il y avait la rue étrangement sourde
au désespoir d'Alice
aux perles de sueurs qui ornaient
son nombril
rendaient humides ses draps de baptiste
la rue les voisins
la mascarade des conventions
il y avait Oreste
le jardin et ses bosquets
Alice et les moissons des saisons fades
au creux de son lit
Alice son cœur qui durcit
gobe les nourrissons
les transperce à la baïonnette
Il y avait la route sombre et muette
les barricades dont Oreste
avait seul le secret
Alice à la peau parfumée de lavande
au cœur de pierre à gober les nourrissons
puis
il y eût Alice
et Oreste
Alice un arc en ciel échevelé
roucoule dans sa gorge
Alice et Oreste
une pluie d'étoiles dans les veines
une pluie d'étoiles leur zèbre la peau

Alice end of an island on an island
at the end of the street
with the street strangely deaf
to her despair
with pearls of sweat adorning
her navel
dampening her cotton sheets
the street the neighbors
the charade of conventions
there was Oreste
the garden and its groves
Alice and the tightness of her life's harvests
in the hollow of her bed
Alice with a heart so hard
it could swallow infants
spear them
there was the dark and mute road
the gates with Oreste alone
holding the key
Alice of the lavender-scented skin
of the heart of stone, swallower of infants
then
there was Alice
and Oreste
Alice a disheveled rainbow
a coo in her throat
Alice and Oreste
fireworks in the veins
fireworks streaking their skin

Ô ma terre

Tu as gardé en otage
l'allégresse de tous mes printemps
ma voix captive
en cette saison
de chuchotements
J'ai gardé en moi ô ma terre
souvenir de tes entrailles inquiètes
ta voix cette flûte emballée

J'ai gardé mémoire de la peur qui assaille tes murs
et la magie têtue
de ce temps malgré tout d'étonnements

Je me souviens
il pleuvait tant d'étoiles la nuit
mais sous tes faux-cils et ton rimmel
il y avait ton regard fatigué
devant les fenêtres sales du temps

En ce temps-là
nous chassions toi et moi
un vent pyromane
qui détruirait
cet apophtegme

Et dans nos tempes en longues traînées de feu
nos rêves distillaient des vertiges
fêtes-dieu rouge-flamboyant

Il pleuvait tant d'étoiles la nuit
pourtant noires et dérisoires

O My Land

You held the joy
of all my springs hostage
my voice captive
in that season
of whispers
I kept within me O my land
memories of your worried guts
your voice this muffled flute

I kept the memory of the fear that besieged your walls
and the stubborn magic
of that time despite every shock

I recall
how the stars shot across the sky
yet beneath your false eyelashes and kohl
there, your weary gaze
facing time's dirty windows

Back then
we chased, you and I,
a pyromaniac wind
that would destroy
this saying

And in our temples in long streaks of fire
raged our dizzy dreams
our holy red festivals

So many stars shot across the night skies
yet our silhouettes

nos silhouettes se confondaient
aux ombres des barbelés
dressés contre les favelas de notre morceau d'Amérique
C'était à Bogota Port-au-Prince ou Rio
les fenêtres de la vie partout
avaient cette teinte sale et tenace
et les jour longs comme des années

À travers ouragans et tempêtes
nous avons tant de fois
toi et moi
vu naître et mourir la vie

Puis à fond de cale cette hantise
d'un miracle
à ton océan j'ai alors légué mes écailles
pour devenir
de tribord à bâbord
lambeau de terre sans testament

J'ai gardé souvenir de ton visage
garrotté par le silence ô ma terre
alors qu'ils t'aspergeaient
de tant de sperme maudit

Tant d'hommes ont sur ta couche
laissé trace de leurs pas
et voilà que la mer elle-même
jour après jour s'obstine à te trahir
Il n'y a désormais
plus un port pour tes chimères

black and pitiful
joined the shadows of the barbed wire
raised against the favelas in our piece of America
It was Bogota Port-au-Prince or Rio
where all the windows of life
had that shade, dirty, stubborn
had days long as years

Through hurricanes and storms
you and I
so often
saw life rise and die

Then in the hold in that haunting
of a miracle
I bequeathed my scales to your ocean
to become
from starboard to port
a piece of land without a will

I kept the image of your face
strangled by silence O my land
with so much cursed sperm
spilled on you

with so many men leaving
their footprints on your bed
and here the sea itself
day after day persists in betraying you
with no more
port for your dreams

Perejil

C'était un matin comme les autres
un matin de belle aube caraïbe
un matin d'octobre

Le soleil comme les autres matins
avait de ses longs doigts dessiné les flancs des mornes
et fait frémir les corolles impatientes des fleurs

Les coqs comme les autres matins
avaient annoncé
aux nantis
les promesses sans frontières
aux parias les labeurs
sans lendemain

Les coqs n'avaient pas annoncé la folie
mais elle avait jailli dans les cannaies
elle avait nom PEREJIL

C'était quelque chose qui rugissait
cris de bêtes aveugles
Comme un océan malade PEREJIL

Elle arrachait sur son passage
bras et têtes d'enfants qui
étonnés
allaient rouler dans les caniveaux
macérer avec la bagasse

Elle avançait PEREJIL

Perejil

It was a morning like any other
a beautiful Caribbean dawn
an October morning

The sun as on other mornings
had drawn the sides of the hills with its long fingers
had made the impatient corollas of the flowers shudder

The roosters as on other mornings
had announced
to the rich
borderless promises
and to outcasts
unending labor

The roosters had yet to announce the madness
that had sprung in the cane-fields
with the name PEREJIL

Something that roared
like the cries of blind beasts
like a sick ocean PEREJIL

Passing it tore off
the astonished arms and heads
of children
which went rolling into the gutters
to steep with the cane syrup

It advanced PEREJIL

la haine à bout de bras
sans entendre les prières fondues dans les cris
et répandait dans les bateyes
une odeur âcre de sang chaud
de sang horrible et gratuit

C'était un matin d'octobre
un matin comme les autres

Le soleil inutile giclait sur les corps entassés
une folie appelée PEREJIL avait transformé des hommes
en cadavres de chiens délaissés

Un ouragan démentiel du nom de PEREJIL
arraché quarante mille vies
dans les éclairs de machettes

Sous un ciel bleu ironique inutile
un ciel beau à faire mal
bleu comme un voile d'épousée

La folie dans les replis du voile
avait germé
gonflé
éclaté
déchiqueté
quarante mille hommes

Ainsi parlent Alciné Louis Joseph Sélome Louidor Antoine
et les autres
la nuit
Lorsque les machettes se taisent

hatred at arm's length
ignoring the prayers fused in the cries
spreading across the bateyes
sharp odor of hot blood
of horrible unjustified blood

It was an October morning
a morning like any other

The useless sun spurt on piled bodies
a madness called PEREJIL had turned men
into cadavers of abandoned dogs

A demented hurricane with the name PEREJIL
ripping away forty thousand lives
in the flash of machetes

Beneath a useless ironic blue sky
a beautiful sky meant to wound
blue as a bridal veil

Madness in the folds of the veil
had taken root
inflated
burst
shredded
forty thousand human beings

So say Alciné Louis Joseph Sélome Louidor Antoine
and the others
the night
the machetes stop talking

la voix effrayée
ils racontent PEREJIL

Sous un ciel caraïbe trop beau
un ciel beau à faire mal
comme une carcasse de viejo
comme des chiens qui n'en finissent pas de crever
ils racontent à leurs enfants congos

Et lorsque la nuit engloutit la canne
comme dans le silence d'un cimetière
quarante mille âmes
dans le vent tiède caraïbe murmurent
PEREJIL PEREJIL
tache fraîche dans notre mémoire

in frightened voices
they tell of PEREJIL

Beneath a too-beautiful Caribbean sky
a sky so beautiful to be awful
like a carcass of a viejo
like dogs who never stop dying
they tell their congo children

And when the night engulfs the cane
as in the silence of a cemetery
forty thousand souls
in the warm Caribbean wind murmur
PEREJIL PEREJIL
stain fresh in our memory

Midi

Midi dans les cités sans nom
sans horloges et
sans heures
toutes les horloges disent MIDI

Midi relent de venin et d'arsenic
de morts à fortes doses

Midi un soleil insolent enflamme une mare
où mijotent des cadavres
de rats et de chiens morts lapidés
une autre cité sans nom
a émergé de la nuit d'hier
elle ressemble aux autres comme sœur
réchauffe ses flancs de carton
ses flancs gris et humides
sur les tas de fientes et d'alluvions

Dans ces maisons aux flancs couverts de lèpre
ces maisons sans nom des cités sans nom
il est toujours Midi
l'heure ou la douleur au ras du sol
rue parfois telle une bête
douleur des ghettos affamés en plein midi
douleur forgée à coups de mépris
rancœur devenue bête à six millions de têtes

Toutes les horloges de toutes les cités sans nom
ont inscrit Midi douleur de l'enfant mort
pour ne pas trop attendre

Noon

Noon in the unnamed cities
without clocks and
without hours
all the clocks read NOON

Noon reeking of venom
and mortal arsenic

Noon an enraged sun setting fire to a pond
simmering with the carcasses
of rats and stoned dogs
another unnamed city
risen from yesterday's night
looking like the others like a sister
heating her cardboard flanks
her faded and damp flanks
on the piles of excrement and alluvium

In these houses with leprous flanks
these unnamed houses in unnamed cities
it is always Noon
the hour in which pain sits at ground level
at times charging like a beast
pain of ghettos hungry at full noon
pain forged in constant contempt
rancor become a beast with six million heads

All the clocks of all the unnamed cities
have written Noon pain of the child
dead for not wanting to wait any more

du vieillard mort pour avoir trop attendu
l'enfant et le vieillard morts
comme le rat et le chien
le rat et le chien morts lapidés
le vieillard et l'enfant morts assassinés
par ce qui refusent le riz et les pois
aux tables branlantes des cités sans nom

MIDI l'heure de Maria et Rosie
qui enterrent l'enfant mort
l'enfant mort dans les bras
sans fleurs ni couronnes
Maria sans passé sans âge
Maria et Rosie sans nom ont poussé
sans savoir pourquoi
dans les ruelles sans noms
des cités sans nom

Midi elles émergent
confondues fille et mère
avec dans les yeux
ces longs chemins de tristesse
comme des années d'agonie
Midi brouillard
dans l'indécence d'un soleil
qui cherche ses réponses
dans les tas de fientes et d'alluvions
elles émergent et la douleur
n'en finit plus de creuser en elles
douleur de tous les enfants et
tous les vieillards morts
cris de multitudes à l'assaut de la vie
douleur en friche

of the old man dead for having waited too long
the child and the old man dead
like the rat and the dog
the rat and the dog stoned
the old man and child murdered
by those denying them rice and peas
at the rickety tables of the cities without names

NOON the hour of Maria and Rosie
who bury the dead child
the dead child in arms
with no flowers no wreaths
Maria with no past no age
Maria and Rosie without names grown
without knowing why they exist
in the alleys without names
in the cities without names

Noon they emerge
indistinguishable daughter mother
in their eyes
the long paths of sorrow
like years of anguish
noon fog
in the indecency of a sun
that seeks its answers
in the piles of excrement and alluvium
they emerge and the pain
doesn't stop digging in them
the pain of all the dead children and
all the dead old ones
cries of the droves fighting with life
fallow pain

douleur sans nom
douleur au poing torche poignard
conque marine pour frapper au cœur
de tous les siècles de douleur

MIDI à tout jamais
aux horloges des cités sans nom
ils ont choisi de cracher
sur les mains tendues
nous choisissons MIDI
nous connaissons déjà depuis si longtemps
cette douleur fraîche et impeccable
de l'aube au crépuscule
et toutes les nuits
chaque nuit
jusqu'à l'aube encore les cris
de la douleur et de Midi
s'emmêlent
douleur du pain
dont on refuse à nos mains rêches
la douceur
la saveur sur nos langues amères

Toutes les horloges
des maisons sans murs
des cités sans nom MIDI
où la vie tous les jours vous surprend
dans cette douleur qui ne surprend plus
souffrance engrangée
qui monte des entrailles de la terre
de ce morceau de terre
amour et déchirure depuis tant de siècles
puisqu'ils ont choisi d'être à jamais

nameless pain
pain like a fist a torch a knife
conch shell to strike at the center
of all the centuries of pain

NOON forever
on the clocks of the nameless cities
they have chosen to spit
on the outstretched hands
we are choosing NOON
knowing already for so long
this fresh and impeccable pain
from dawn to dusk
and all the nights
every night
until dawn and still more cries
of pain and of Noon
mixing
pain of bread
denied to our rough hands
the sweetness
the flavor on our bitter tongues

All the clocks
of the wall-less houses
of the unnamed cities NOON
where everyday life surprises you
in this pain that no longer surprises you
suffering built up
rising from the entrails of the earth
from this piece of earth
love and heartbreak for so many centuries
because they have chosen to be forever

flibustiers pirates banquistes
saltimbanques affameurs pyromanes
nous aussi nous choisissons

Midi l'heure des choix sans riz et pois
Midi hors des murs de nos cités sans nom
Midi s'inquiète comme nos tripes
Midi s'agite comme nos bras
Midi dévale dans nos veines
Midi brûle brasier
Midi de poudre
Midi de sang
Midi tempête
Midi hurle avec Maria et Rosie
l'enfant et le vieillard morts
le marché qui brûle aux trousses des pyromanes
        Toutes les horloges calcinées ont inscrit MIDI

filibusterers pirates flatterers
acrobats starvers pyromaniacs
we, we also choose

Noon hour of choices without rice without peas
Noon beyond the walls of our unnamed cities
Noon worried like our guts
Noon shaking like our arms
Noon hurtling into our veins
Noon firebrand
Noon of powder
Noon of blood
Noon storm
Noon screaming with Maria and Rosie
the child and old man dead
the market burning in the wake of pyromaniacs
        All the burned clocks proclaiming NOON

À mes fils

Griserie et amertume de marronnage
se refusent à abandonner notre sang
nous vîmes le jour papillon de nuit pour tenter d'attraper
ne serait-ce qu'une étoile
elles filent sans cesse
coquines
avant que sous nos paupières
n'éclose aucune espérance

À travers les siècles des siècles depuis tant de siècles
nous avons vu passer les printemps
nous les avons de loin contemplés
comme si nous voulions
qu'ils nous disent
nous révèlent
quelque amer et douloureux secret

À travers les siècles des siècles
le poids de l'injure écumant dans la gorge nous courbe l'échine
amertume et ivresse du marronnage empoisonnent notre sang
leur âme reste blanche
saisie
sous les banquises millénaires

Dans quelle voûte de quel ciel
de peur qu'on ne l'assassine
notre cœur allons-nous enfermer?

To My Sons

The wild freedom and bitterness of marooning
refuses to leave our blood
we are born night butterflies
hoping to catch even the smallest stars
which slip away
endless and unruly
before any hope
blooms
under our eyelids

From century to century for so many centuries
springs have passed us by
we have studied them from afar
as if they could
share
make clear
some bitter painful secret

From century to century
insults deep and foaming in the throat bend us
the bitterness and inebriation of marooning poisons our blood
while their souls remain frozen
trapped
beneath ancient ice floes

In which vault of which sky
of fear
will we lock up our hearts?

Posons le pied

Animées de cette fureur de l'amante trahie
posons le pied
ancrons le talon
catapultons
la rage au ventre
les monstres repus
de tant de violences et
de félonies

Les paumes sur les oreilles
sourdes demeurons
aux grognements des chacals

Oyez femmes aux mamelles fécondes et pleines
affûtez lattes et yatagans
hyènes et coyotes hurlent à la lune
se repaîtront de vos douces chairs
assècheront la dernière perle de votre lait

Hyènes et coyotes
la conscience enfiévrée
ivres de folies et de parjures
renient haut et fort

Comme un navire foudroyé
notre ventre chavire
notre sexe en berne vomit
les prières des fossoyeurs
et leurs phallus-galères
nos entrailles désormais refusent
le vagissement horrible des monstres

Let's Put the Foot Down

Fueled by the fury of a betrayed lover
Let's put the foot down
anchor the heel
catapult
the rage in the belly
the monsters sated
with so much violence
with so many crimes

Hands over ears
staying deaf
to the growls of jackals

Hear women full-breasted and fertile
sharpen their slats and knives
hyenas and coyotes howling at the moon
to feast on your sweet flesh
to dry the last pearl of your milk

Hyenas and coyotes
with fevered minds
drunk with madness and lies
renouncing loud and clear

Like a blasted ship
belly capsized
our sex sunken hurling back
the prayers of gravediggers
and their phallus-galleys
our guts from this moment refusing
the horrible whine of monsters

Pour Toi

La nuit s'étire jusqu'à demain
nous garderons les volets clos
je serai ton étoile nouvellement née
tu confondras mes rayons

La nuit s'étire
comme un doux souvenir
comme la joie tout à l'air si fragile
mais je serai ta rivière ton ailleurs
un éclat d'île rien que pour toi
tu oublieras ta faim

Sybarite
je t'offrirai mes soupirs en quartiers de lune
je serai souï-manga et de mon bec habile
j'étonnerai ton sang

For You

The night stretches until day
we will keep the shutters closed
I will be your new-born star
you will mix up my rays

The night stretches
like a sweet memory
like joy everything seems so fragile
but I will be your river your elsewhere
an island glow just for you
you will forget your hunger

Sybarite
I will offer you my sighs in slices of moon
I will be a souï-manga and with my skillful beak
I will amaze your blood

Île Indigo

Île indigo
le jour ronge ses freins
la nuit mûrit de fébriles courroux
les premières amours
ne s'aventurent plus dans les bosquets
et ce poulpe de perdition
ce poulpe à longue barbe
aux visages maculés de scrofules
s'agrippe à ce qui reste de toi

Île indigo
la valse folle de perdition tourbillonne encore
derrière les grilles et les murs hérissés de tessons
l'aïeule abandonnée rend son dernier soupir

Indigo Island

Indigo island
the day chomps at the bit
the night ripens with feverish wrath
the first loves
no longer venture into thickets
and the octopus of damnation
this octopus with its long beard
with its faces smeared with scrofula
holds onto what's left of you

Indigo island
the mad waltz of hell still whirls
behind grids and walls bristling with shards
where the abandoned ancestor takes her last breath

La ville

Les gens errent et se croisent
les femmes et leurs jupes criardes
font gonfler l'angoisse et ses poings tendus
la foule muette
a de ces mouvements nerveux et prodigieux
des vagues furieuses enfourchent le Quai Colomb

Le vent qui se lève emmène des senteurs de fiel
c'est le manchot qui a libéré ce que cachait l'écluse
non c'est le cul de jatte
ou plutôt cette mère
qui voit les flots engloutir quatre petites filles
vêtues de taffetas rose et blanc

Le vent sème des nuages lourds de sang
Pour apaiser cette brûlure du rêve
toujours vivant sous la cendre

Qui a libéré l'écluse criera-t-on à la ronde?
ni le manchot qui en plus est un cul de jatte
ni le cul de jatte qui en plus est aveugle
ni la mère qui sur son sein
fait revivre une photo
un premier sourire
et frémit
au souvenir des lèvres goulues
du dernier-né sur ses seins

Le vent a délaissé le parfum grisant
du poisson et du lard frits

The Town

People wander and cross paths
women in loud skirts
make anxiety billow its outstretched fists
the mute crowd
has the nervous and prodigious movements
of the furious waves straddling the Quai Colomb

The rising wind bears the scent of gall
the one-armed man has released what the lock concealed
no it's the legless man
no it's a mother
seeing the waves bear off four small girls
dressed in pink and white taffeta

The wind sows clouds heavy with blood
to soothe this burn of a dream
still alive beneath the ash

Who released the lock? everyone shouts
not the armless man who moreover is legless
or the legless man who moreover is blind
or the mother who on her breast
brings to life a photo
a first smile
and shudders
at the memory of greedy lips
and the last-born suckling at her breast

The wind has forsaken the heady scent
of fried fish and meat

il habille la ville de braises et de tisons
La fumée emprunte ce visage dément des marées en détresse
l'écluse déborde et n'apaise nulle soif
au galop les vagues sur le Quai Colomb

dressing the city with charcoal and embers
the smoke borrows the insane face of distressed tides
the lock overflows and quenches no thirst
galloping atop the waves of the Quai Colomb

MAGGY DE COSTER

Les versets simplifiés du soleil levant |
The simplified verses of the rising sun

1

Résiste . . . marche haut les mains sur les voies libératrices
Fuis la compagnie des moqueurs malséants
Sois comme l'arbre qui plonge ses racines dans les ruisseau
Qui désaltère les assoiffés du bonheur de vivre
Cet arbre qui prodigue son ombre au promeneur harassé

Le vent dissipe des fragments de vérités occultées qui parviennent
Aux oreilles attentives mais les aveugles d'esprit
Les précipitent dans l'hypogée de leurs pensées irréversibles

Dans le vortex des jours demeurent en suspension tant de points
Semblables à des grains de sable emportés par des marées

2

Que dire de tant de pensées stériles
Qui parsèment les lobes du cerveau
L'absurde gangrène les espaces de vie
Le verbe se fige dans le vide des convenances
La force des idées se perd dans les soubassements de la colère

Les dires de coryphée se diluent dans les méandres
                    du désenchantement
Point de garde-de fou dans l'avant-scène: le péril se décrète
La nuit chasse le jour et tout recommence

La demande est instante
L'instant n'attend pas
La coupe se vide dans le vide
Et le vide se remplit du contenant et du contenu

1

March hands up on freedom's road . . . Resist
Break from the crooked mockers
Be like the tree that sinks its roots into the stream
Slaking those thirsty for life's rays
Tree that shares its shade with the hassled walker

The wind scatters fragments of hidden truths that reach
Attentive ears but those blind of mind
Bury truth in the ground of their irreparable thoughts

In the vortex of days, so many points remain suspended
Like grains of sand swept away by the tides

2

What to say about so many bare thoughts
That dot the brain's lobes
The absurd infecting life's living rooms
The verb freezing in the absence of decorum
The force of ideas being lost in the basements of rage

The words of leaders grow weak and meander in bitterness
No guardrails before the curtain, the danger is decreed
Night drives out day and everything begins again

The demand is instant
The moment does not wait
The cup empties into the void
And the void fills itself with container and contained

3

Sur ordonnance de la pensée positive
Je m'en vais siéger sur la plus haute montagne
Je mettrai en déroute les idées noires
Avec le bouclier de l'amour
Je vaincrai les affres de la peur
Mon chant de victoire s'élèvera dans les airs
Et les fluides de mon être graviteront
Autour du champ spectral des rêves

4

La clameur des innocents
N'ébranle point leurs assaillants
À la conscience aveugle et déréglée
Véritables ensembles vides à l'échelle mathématique
Signataires d'un pacte sanguinaire inscrit dans la perpétuité
D'un règne abominable et scellé dans la vacuité de l'esprit

5

Je tends d'oreille pour écouter le souffle épique du vent
Il dédie la mélopée des hirondelles de mer
Aux marins happés par la furie des vagues
Les yeux rivés sur le firmament je découvre
La parade de l'arc-en-ciel et des rais de soleil après l'averse
Et le parfum de l'humus se révèle à mon l'odorat
Je goûte au sel de la joie en offrant une légère caresse
Aux éphémères coquelicots des champs

3

With orders to think positively
I will sit on the highest mountain
I will rout the dark thoughts
With love's shield
I will conquer fear's pangs
My victory song will rise in the air
The fluids of my being will circulate
On the spectral field of dreams

4

The cries of innocents
Do not shake their assailants
To the blind and disordered conscience
Emptiness on a grand scale
Signatories of a bloody pact written to last
Of an awful reign sealed in the blankness of spirit

5

I strain to hear the epic breath of the wind
It dedicates the melody of sea swallows
To sailors caught in the fury of waves
Eyes fixed on the firmament I find
The rainbow's display, the rays of the sun after the rain
The scent of the earth reveals itself to me
I taste the salt of joy, granting a light stroke
To the fleeting poppies of the fields

6

Je m'enivre de l'opium de la nuit
Pour gravir le versant onirique de ma vie
Et mes pensées bohèmes se libèrent
Des hémisphères de mon cerveau
Pour relier les hémisphères terrestres en perpétuels conflits
Mais la réalité se révèle comme un transi
qu'il faut fuir à toutes jambes

7

J'assemble les vertèbres des mots
Pour construire une pyramide de pensées
salvatrices en faveur des âmes en péril
Je dissèque avec minutie les songes de ma vie
Pour y trouver les trésors immanents
à décalquer d'un mouvement dextre
Augurant des choses sensées

8

Aérienne, je navigue d'espace en espace
De la munificence de la nature
Je puise la sève de mon existence
Je remplis ma besace des fruits de l'amitié
glanés à chaque étape
Je franchis les frontières
et les transperce avec ma plume
Des idées plurielles jaillissent
pour enfin s'incruster dans le tissue de mes jours
comme un tatouage indélébile

6

I get drunk on the opium of the night
To climb the dreamlike side of my life
Bohemian thoughts breaking free
From the hemispheres of my brain
To connect the earthly halves in endless war
But reality makes itself known, a chill
to be fled at full speed

7

I gather the vertebrae of words
To build a pyramid of restoring thought
favoring imperiled souls
I dissect with care the dreams of my life
To find in them innate treasures
to trace with dexterous gesture
the portent of sensible things

8

Aerial, I sail from space to space
From nature's bounty
I draw the sap of my being
I fill my bag with the fruits of friendship
gathered at every stop
I cross borders
and pierce them with my pen
Such ideas spring forth
to become fixed in the fabric of my days
like indelible tattoos

9

Capter en douceur ces instants de lumière
Que projette le ciel par moments
Ces instants se dessinent comme des feux follets
Ou des formes folâtres voletant à la vitesse variable
Instants gradués à l'échelle des heures
Et qui défient la permanence de la monotonie

10

Dans le champ des connaissances
Les épis du savoir se raréfient
Il n'y croît que des herbes folles
La conscience s'appauvrit comme une montagne pelée
Le filet du pêcheur est vide
Sa barque a fait naufrage au large du rêve
Effaré, il laisse errer son regard livide
Encourra-t-il la perpétuité de l'infortune?

11

Comme des herbes folles dans le parterre de la déraison
Les erreurs se découvrent dans les pages détachées du livre des aveux
Alors il ne reste qu'à céder à l'extrême pulsion du verbe agir
Pour s'épargner de l'ordalie de feu
Et laisser ondoyer l'oriflamme de l'amour reviviscent sur le pavillon
                des cœurs,
remparts contre les vanités et l'aliénation conjuguées

9

Capture gently these moments of light
That the sky at times projects
Moments drawing themselves like will-o'-the-wisps
Playful forms flying at variable speed
Moments moving across the scale of hours
Unfixed by monotony

10

In the field of knowledge
Ears of knowledge grow scarce
Weeds push up there
Consciousness as needy as a bare mountain
The fisherman's net is empty
His boat shipwrecked far from the dream
Afraid, he lets his pallid gaze wander
Will he always suffer?

11

Like weeds in unreason's bed
Faults crop up in the loose pages of the book of confessions
Succumbing to the sharp urge of the verb to act is what remains
Saving oneself from the fire's heat
Letting love's lifted banner wave over the pavilion of hearts,
ramparts against conjugal vanities and distance

12

Comment assainir les sentiers broussailleux
et retrouver les statuts des jours de paix?
Je cache les pétales de joie dans les profondeurs de mon être
pour les épargner de la flétrissure
Je conjure à voix basse les revers du quotidien
Je lève ma coupe à la gloire de l'esprit sain
et au clair de jour en extase je sautille

Tant de fois inconnue à moi-même
je frisonne d'effroi au trot de mes pensées
dans l'antichambre de mon cerveau
Quel Prince convoquer à nos conciliabules
pour donner le ton à la plaidoirie des faibles?
Ô nature immarcescible je t'adjure de nous être favorable!

13

Quand la terre disparaîtra
Je gémirai dans les limbes
Les souvenirs du passé seront portés disparus
La vie sera-t-elle aux abonnés absents?
Quoi qu'en pensent d'aucuns
Le temps continuera sa course inexorable
Et chacun aura peut-être fait son temps
sans avoir rien fait de son temps
Est-ce le temps qui nous marque
ou nous qui le marquons?

12

How to clear trails of brush
and find the statutes of days of peace?
I hide joy's petals deep in my being
to keep them from withering
In a quiet voice I call up life's disappointments
I raise my cup to the glory of sanity
And in daylight leap with joy

So often unaware
I have shivered with fear as my thoughts trotted
In the front chamber of my brain
Which Prince to summon to our meetings
To set the tone in defense of the weak?
O unfading nature, be favorable to us!

13

When the earth disappears
I will moan in limbo
Memories of the past will be carried off
Will life too be absent?
Despite it all
Time will continue its inexorable course
With each perhaps having had their time
having done nothing with their time
Is it time that marks us
Or we who mark it?

14

À la saison des amours folles
Je danserai la gigue sur Le Pont des Arts
À la pleine lune
Je m'embarquerai sur le lac Majeur
Je chanterai la chanson des étoiles
Dans l'allégresse des moments
Je signerai un pacte de sérénité avec les anges du Paradis
Et dans la pérennité je règnerai sur la moitié du ciel

15

Comme des pas sur le sable mouvant
Je trace le diagramme de mes chimères
Pour ne pas verser dans la procrastination
Le vent finira par sécher les gouttes superfétatoires
Qui débordent du calice de mes pleurs
Et les jours me feront l'aumône de leur clémence
Pour m'épargner de la démence
Et sans crainte je vivrai d'amour et d'espérance

16

Suturer cent fois la morsure du temps
Pour conjurer la mort sûre
Et ne pas prendre le mors aux dents
Quand s'écroule le radeau en mer étale

Ne pas laisser se répandre des libations de sang
Ne pas laisser fleurir des sentences de haine
Mais aux trois coups de brigadier
Laisser entrer le messager en scène
Pour faire allégeance à l'amour

14

In the season of mad love
I will dance the jig on the Pont des Arts
At full moon
I will embark on Lake Maggiore
I will sing the song of the stars
In the joy of moments
I will sign a pact of serenity with the angels of Paradise
And forever rule half the sky

15

Like footsteps on quicksand
I draw the diagram of my illusions
To avoid procrastination
The wind will in due time dry the extra drops
That overflow from the chalice of my tears
And the days will offer me the alms of their mercy
To save me from madness
Free of fear I will live on love and hope

16

Stitch up time's bite a hundred times
Ward off sure death
Don't take the bit between the teeth
When the raft collapses in the calm sea

Don't offer libations of blood
Or allow hate's grammar to grow
When the three shots ring out
Let the messenger enter the scene
To pledge allegiance to love

17

Dans la gamme de mes rêves
J'ai inscrit le refrain de l'Amour
En allégro à fredonner avec entrain

Sur le parchemin de ma vie
J'ai écrit les versets du soleil
À réciter avec allégresse

Sur l'échiquier de mon cœur
Les pions forment une haie d'espoir
Pour âme en peine

18

Je veux laisser pousser dans mon champ
Les glaïeuls aux couleurs de la victoire
Victoire-repoussoir du glaive de la guerre
Glaive-faucheur de l'innocence
Et déversoir de sang dans les entrailles de la terre
Terre-rempart des sacrificateurs

Quand auront germé les semences tardives
Combien serons-nous pour la fête de la moisson?

19

Environnés par le spectre de la mort
Engendrés par les guerres
Pourchassés par le vent du désespoir
Ils se fraient un passage dans les ténèbres
Ils s'avancent en titubant

17

In the notes of my dreams
I wrote Love's refrain
In allegro to hum intensely

On the parchment of my life
I wrote the verses of the sun
To recite with joy

On the chessboard of my heart
The pawns form a hedge of hope
For the suffering soul

18

I want to grow in my field
Gladioli the colors of Victory
Victory foil of the sword of war
Harvest sword of innocence
Channel of blood to the bowels of the earth
Earth-bulwark of those who offer sacrifices

When will the late seeds sprout
How many will we be for the harvest festival?

19

Surrounded by the specter of death
Spawned by wars
Carried by the winds of despair
They make their way through the darkness
Staggering forward

Avides de paix et de lumière
À la recherche d'un asile sûr

Mais là-bas se dressent d'infâmes murailles géantes
À contourner ou à franchir
Sans s'affranchir de la peur de l'inconnu
La fatigue les lamine sans merci
La faim leur entaille les tripes
La soif fleur tenaille le gosier
Et autour d'eux sans cesse rôde l'épouvante

Le point de non-retour est déjà atteint
Mais quand les exterminateurs seront-ils à jamais anéantis?

20

M'abreuver à la source de l'Infini
Décrypter le rêve des dauphins
Dans les nuitées océanes
Avant de m'endormir à jamais
Dans les entrailles de la terre

Je caresse ma chimère
Vivace elle demeure
Elle épouse la forme de mes nuits
Mon cœur palpite d'impatience
Un autre jour se lève et je me retrouve
Encore avec elle comme une amie fidèle

Longing for peace and light
Seeking a haven

But the infamous giant walls stand there
To circumvent or cross
Carrying the fear of the unknown
Fatigue tears them down with no mercy
Hunger pierces their guts
Thirst grips their throats
And around them terror constantly roams

The point of no return has already been reached
When will the exterminators be forever destroyed?

20

To drink at the source of the Infinite
Deciphering the dolphin's dream
In the ocean's nights
Before forever falling asleep
In the womb of the earth

I embrace my chimera
Long may she live
She marries the shape of my nights
My heart throbs with expectation
Another day dawns and brings me back
Still with her like a faithful friend

21

Ne nous livrons pas en pâture à la morosité
Ne plions pas encore bagages
Malaisé est le chemin
Mais la Victoire est au bout du bout
Sous l'égide de Niké nous arborerons
L'étendard de la victoire
Et nous irons en nombre festoyer sur l'Olympe

22

Moi le phénix des temps modernes
Je renais avec mon âme d'enfant
Je parcours les contrées lyriques
Et avec mes plumes renaissantes
Je réécris les contes des mille et une nuits enjolivés d'amour et de soie
Je transporte les parodies du vent
sur le versant des collines enneigées
Je m'enivre du miel des lunes d'été
Je m'enrobe dans les plis des champs de blé vert d'espérance
Et je bois dans le calice des rosées du matin
Avant la danse macabre des corbeaux au lever du soleil

23

Je sillonne les plaines infertiles
Où s'exécutent les joutes mémorielles du silence
Je partage avec les goélands les confidences des ruisseaux
revanchards jadis jugulés par les puissances perfides de la terre
Qui finiront par subir la sublime sentence des sylphes
Je me restaure des instants de bonheur puisés dans l'écorce
                    des souvenirs

21

Let's not indulge in gloom
Let's not give up yet
The way is hard
But Victory stands at its end
Under Nike's aegis we will bear its flag
And go in numbers to feast on Olympus

22

I am the modern phoenix
Reborn with a child's soul
I travel the lyrical lands
With my reborn feathers
I rewrite the tales of a thousand and one nights adorned with
              love and silk
I carry the parodies of the wind
On the slopes of snow-covered hills
I get drunk on the honey of summer moons
I wrap myself in the folds of hope's green wheat fields
And drink from the chalice of morning dews
Before the death dance of crows at sunrise

23

I roam the infertile plains
Where memorial battles of silence take place
I share the secrets of streams with the gulls
Revengers once restrained by the treacherous forces of the earth
Who will end up suffering the sublime judgement of the sylphs
I restore myself with moments of joy drawn from the bark
              of memories

Sur mon passage je cueille les grappes d'espoir qui dépassent
de l'enclos du destin
Avant que ne tombe la nuit sur les allées de ma vie

24

Archaïsme du verbe révélé par la réverbération des vertèbres fracassées
Frissonnement des herbes folles coiffant les prés solitaires
Rêves fossilisés dans les nuits incantatoires des amours
Incarnation de la folie dans les lobes de la pensée
Réplique des moment non verbalisés
Consomption des vœux inexprimés
Crémation des esprits illuminés.

Infinitude du soi glissant sur la pente savonneuse des chimères
Invalidation du corpus de la déraison
Damnation des âmes enchaînées dans le passage des passions
puissantes
Lacération de l'innocence par le vol des vautours
Onde de choc dans le sérail des peintres
peignant la permanence de la peur

Confusion des sentiments rougis du sang des anges
En arrosage des jardins périssables
Conjuration des étoiles immobiles dans un ciel consterné

25

Je me découvre sur la terre des vivants
et me demande pourquoi je suis ici-bas
Les jours se succèdent et mes *pourquoi* ne cèdent guère aux
chantages de mon être

On my way I gather the clusters of hope which extend beyond
destiny's gates
Before night falls on the alleys of my life

24

The ancient trait of the verb made clear in the reverberations
of shattered vertebrae
The rustling of the wild grass covering the lonely meadows
Fossilized dreams in incantatory nights of love
Embodiment of madness in the lobes of thought
Replica of unspoken moments
Consummation of unexpressed wishes
Cremation of enlightened spirits

Infinity of the self, sliding down the slippery slope of chimeras
Invalidation of the corpus of unreason
Damnation of souls chained in the passage of powerful passions
Laceration of innocence by the flight of vultures
Shock wave in the seraglio of painters
combing the permanence of fear

Confusion of feelings reddened with the blood of angels
In watering the fragile gardens
The conjuring of motionless stars in a dismayed sky

25

I discover myself in the land of the living
and wonder why I'm down here
The days follow one another, my *whys* hardly yield to the
blackmail of my being

n'accordent non plus nulle concession à la récurrence de ma curiosité
ni à la dérivation de mes pensées scabreuses

Dans l'attente de la Vérité
je me réfugie dans la base des *comment*
où je tente de construire l'édifice de ma vie dans l'éviction des artéfacts
mais dans le champ des possibles

26

L'infâme loge la vengeance au creuset de son être
   et s'enivre du sang des innocents
    qu'il verse sur l'autel du fanatisme
Et dans l'obscur de sa pensée mûrit
le plan de destruction massive des esprits libres
Ses mains sont souillures de crimes parfaits
Pure orchestration des sacrificateurs entichés d'horreur
Opération macabre brodée d'archaïsme
Véritable antireflet de la modernité

27

Les ténèbres déploient leur voile
   Sur la façade du jour
Où l'araignée sans répit tissait sa toile
Ouvrage au long cours

Elle rêve d'éclaircie pour l'achever
Avant que ne tombe la prescription du temps

Libre et sans bagages l'oiseau voyage
Et parcourt l'immensité de la voûte azurée
Volera-t-il un jour au secours de ceux qui
À pas perdus cherchent le chemin des étoiles?

nor do they grant concession to my recurring questions
or the diversion of my scabrous thoughts

Awaiting the Truth
I take refuge in the basics of *how*
where I try to build the house of my life in the removal of relics,
in the realm of what can be

26

Evil lodges vengeance in the core of his own being
   and gets drunk on the blood of the innocent
    poured on the altar of fanaticism
And in the darkness of his thoughts ripens
the plan for the great destruction of free spirits
His hands are stained with perfect crimes
The pure orchestration of the sacrificers steeped in horror
Macabre operation embroidered with archaism
True anti-reflection of modernity

27

The darkness spreads its veil
   On the face of the day
Where the tireless spider weaves her web
Her long-term work

She dreams of the sun for its completion
Before time runs out

Free and un-heavy the bird travels
Crossing the immensity of the azure vault
Will he fly one day to help
The lost, those seeking the way to the stars?

28

Mon esquif cingle vers la rade du jour
        contre vents et marées
avant la retraite paisible du soleil
Il contourne la joyeuse bande de mouettes
En escale sur des récifs géants

En retard de phase
Les messagers du ciel
Ne délivrent pas à temps
Les missives des anges
Aux travailleurs de la mer

Les éléments délogent les terriens
        sans préavis
Et la terre se fait une joie indicible
De leur ouvrir grand son ventre
Pour le dernier festin

29

L'horreur étale ses tentacules
Et pénètre dans l'embrasure de nos villes
Comme une vague en furie
Elle surprend et engloutit toute âme en fête:
        foule en liesse
          enfants à la mamelle
        ou paisibles passants
Elle se réplique comme les saisons et se duplique à l'infini
Mais qui verbalisera la souffrance des innocents
dont la mort violente a étouffé les cris?

28

My skiff sails toward the day's harbor
        against winds and tides
before the peaceful setting of the sun
It bypasses the merry band of seagulls
Laying over on giant reefs

Late
The sky's messengers
Deliver late
The letters from the angels
To the workers of the sea

The elements displace the earthlings
        with no warning
And the earth rejoices indescribably
In opening its belly to them
For the last feast

29

Horror spreads its tentacles
It enters the doorway of our cities
Like a raging wave
It surprises and engulfs every soul in celebration:
        cheering crowd
        infant at the breast
        peaceful passers-by
It replicates itself like the seasons and duplicates itself ad infinitum
But who will speak the suffering of the innocent
whose cries have been snuffed out by their violent deaths?

30

J'attends que vienne le jour à pas feutrés
colmater les brèches laissées par l'ennemi du bien
J'attends que le soleil vienne en fanfare
sertir de ses rayons le côté pile de la terre
J'attends que la mer vienne me dorloter
avec le tremolo de ses vagues en goguette
J'attends que la lune vienne épouser mes rêves
dans la nuit du solstice d'été
J'attends que le vent vienne sécher mes pleurs de son souffle
                    frémissant
J'attends le sacre de la première hirondelle du dernier printemps

31

L'ombre trace lentement son chemin
Après le passage du soleil
Et les frêles épis frémissent au souffle du vent

Je me dérobe au silence de la nuit
Et me réfugie dans l'antre de mes pensées
J'invoque l'éclat tutélaire d'Altaïr
À l'acmé de mes sentiments

Et se dessine en filigrane la trame de l'espoir
Que j'abrite sous l'auvent d'une saison nouvelle

30

I wait for the day to come quietly
closing the gaps left by the enemy of good
I wait for the sun's arrival with fanfare
to set the hidden face of the earth with its rays
I wait for the sea to pamper me
with the tremolo of its waves in a spree
I wait for the moon to marry my dreams
on the night of the summer solstice
I wait for the wind to dry my tears
with its quivering breath
I wait for the coronation of the first swallow of the last spring

31

The shadow slowly makes its way
After the sun has passed
And the frail ears of corn quiver in the breath of the wind

I hide from the silence of the night
And take refuge in the den of my thoughts
I summon Altaïr's guiding light
At the height of my feelings

And the thread of hope emerges
I shelter it beneath the awning of a new season

32

L'été exhale ses complaints dans la grille des jours
Une nouvelle page volante de plaintes se remplit
Un chapitre se referme sur les clauses du désespoir
Que de rêves brisés au matin dans les soupiraux!

Un autre jour se lève
Mais demeurent présentes sur la grève
Les traces de sang des innocents

Il court tant de bruits dans les parages du vide
Tant de sons discordants remplissent les espaces libres
Comme des épaves délaissées sur les chemins malaisés

La geste mémorielle ne comble pas la béance des souffrances
Ne répare pas non plus la toile trouée par l'éclat des forfaits
Voire moduler la pensée perverse des actionneurs de la
machine infernale

33

Mes pensées déambulent à pas feutrés
Dans les profondeurs de la nuit
Quand résonnent les pas perdus du silence
Dans l'alcôve de mon âme inassouvie
Je voyage dans la galaxie de mes rêves
Pour aller quérir les semences des étoiles
Que je planterai dans l'ogive de mon jardin
À la lune montante

32

Summer exhales its complaints in the trellis of days
A new loose page of complaints fills up
A chapter closes on the clauses of despair
So many dreams shattered in the morning in the vents!

Another day breaks
But remains at the shoreline
Bloodstains of the innocent

So much noise around the void
So many discordant sounds fill the empty spaces
Like abandoned wrecks on uneasy paths

The memorial gesture does not fill the gap of suffering
Nor does it repair the canvas punctured in the explosion of bundles
Or even modulate the perverse thoughts of the drivers of the
                              infernal machine

33

My thoughts wander softly
In the depths of the night
When the lost footsteps of silence resound
In the alcove of my unsatisfied soul
I travel in the galaxy of my dreams
To fetch the seeds of the stars
That I will plant in the arch of my garden
At the rising moon

34

Souffle le vent de la terreur
Disparaît la récolte de l'amour
Et se brise la vie

Les liens de l'horreur
Enchaînent le mendiant de l'espérance
Et du ciel tombe la rosée en guise de larmes

Dans le profil des jours se distingue
La marche de l'hécatombe
des âmes insoumises
et la colère se fait ténor dans l'agora

35

Les cadavres au couchant dérivent dans la frénésie des fous
Comme des pierres qui n'amassent pas mousse
Ou comme les proies de l'ombre
À l'ubac du tertre solitaire
Où les heures noires se décalquent dans l'ossature de nos vies
Comme une douche froide dans la transe des soliloqueurs

36

Le patient fredonne son chant monotone
Dans l'attente de la dégustation du vin de l'espoir
Le souffle puissant du vent fait chavirer la barque
De l'amour en escale sur les rives de l'incertitude

Aux nocturnes des noceurs s'invite la folie
Elle résiste à tout bouclier et fait flèche de tout bois
Invincible elle se veut et ne rate guère sa cible

34

The wind of terror blows
The harvest of love is gone
Life breaks

The links of horror
Chain the beggar of hope
From the sky falls the dew in the guise of tears

The advance of the slaughter
Stands out in the march of days
Rebellious souls
and anger become the tenor of the agora

35

Corpses at sunset drift in a mad frenzy
Like stones that gather no moss
Like the shadow's prey
To the north-facing slope of the solitary land
Where the dark hours trace themselves in the bones of our lives
Like a cold shower of the soliloquist's trance

36

The patient hums a monotonous song
Awaiting the taste of the wine of hope
The strong blast of the wind capsizes the boat
Of love at a stopover on uncertainty's shores

Madness invites herself to the revelers' nocturnes
Resisting any shield, pulling out the stops
Invincible, she wants to live and hardly misses her mark

37

Splendide est la colline au soleil levant
Allons-y que je vous déclare la Paix
Nous prendrons pour témoins les oliviers millénaires
Et la candide colombe nous fera don d'une de ses plumes
Pour sceller nos accords perpétuels sur des feuilles de vigne vierge
À l'encre de nos cœurs pour un nouveau départ

À la guerre nous donnerons une sépulture
Et nous érigerons des citadelles de lumière
Pour les rescapés des ténèbres

38

Des larmes d'adieu pour toi ma cousine Minerve
Trop tôt partie nous laissant tous orphelins de ta présence
La barque de nos pleurs cingle vers le ciel
Auquel nous demandons l'aumône de son réconfort
Lieu-dit de la planète des anges où tu t'es envolée
O funeste envolée sans escale vers l'espace de non-retour

39

Le parfum de l'absence me suffoque
Let mots se sont perdus sur le chemin de l'attente
Mes jours s'arrosent de pleurs torrentiels

Je m'en vais dans le brouillard convoquer mon étoile
Pour vivifier mon cœur avec la myrrhe de ses mots
Arroser la plaine de mon existence de pluies fertiles
Lambrisser de douceur l'édifice de ma vie
Et de bonheur allonger mes jours

37

Splendid is the hill in the rising sun
Let's go there so I may declare peace to you
We will take as witnesses the thousand-year-old olive trees
And the candid dove will offer us one of her feathers
To seal our perpetual agreements on virgin vine leaves
In the ink of our hearts for a new start

We will give a burial to war
And build citadels of light
For the survivors of darkness

38

Farewell tears for you my cousin Minerva
Gone too soon leaving us orphaned of your presence
The boat of our tears sways toward the sky
From whom we ask the alms of its comfort
Site of the planet of angels where you flew
O fatal straight flight toward the space of no return

39

The scent of absence suffocates me
The words have been lost on the path of waiting
My days are watered with torrential tears

I go in the fog to summon my star
To quicken my heart with the myrrh of its words
To water the plain of my being with fertile rains
To panel the house of my life with sweetness
And with happiness lengthen my days

40

Embaumons de nos passions l'âme des forêts en péril
Embrasons d'Amour des tissus fragiles de l'humanité
Sous le regard luminescent de Cassiopée
Achevons la symphonie inachevée des disparus
Et des versets simplifiés du soleil levant
Comblons le vide laissé par l'absence

40

Let us embalm with our passions the soul of imperiled forests
Let us embrace the fragile fabrics of humanity with Love
Beneath the luminescent gaze of Cassiopeia
Let us finish the unfinished symphony of the missing
And with the simplified verses of the rising sun
Fill the void left by the absence

Notes

"What Water Wouldn't I Dry"
the poem's title refers both to the deadly floods in Gonaïves and to tears; *lwa* refers to the gods of the Haitian voudou religion.

"I Said"
Tunapuna, a town in Trinidad; *Lascahobas* and *Port-Margot* are Haitian cities.

"Incandescences"
daïva, a Creolized version of the English word *diver; bonbon sirop,* a spiced sugar-cane cake or cookie.

"Brasero"
brasero or *bracero* refers to a Haitian cane cutter usually found working in the Dominican Republic.

"Blues for Azania"
Azania, the indigenous name applied to parts of southern Africa; situated off the coast of South Africa, *Roben Island* housed the notorious prison in which the anti-apartheid activist Nelson Mandela was held for many years; *Xhosa* refers to a language indigenous to parts of Southern Africa, and to members of a South African people; *Madiba,* the title of respect and Thembu clan name for Nelson Mandela; a *bantustan* was a territory set aside for Black inhabitants under South Africa's policy of apartheid; *the gray of Orange* alludes to the Southern Africa Boer republic of the 19th century; *Brandfort,* the remote town that was home to the anti-apartheid activist Winnie Mandela during her imprisonment and banishment by South Africa's national party government; *Soweto,* the township of Johannesburg, which became a center of anti-apartheid campaigns.

"La Gésine"
gésine, a traditional reference to a woman about to give birth.

"Sources Chaudes"
Sources Chaudes refers to a section in the Moron commune of Jérémie Arrondissement, in Grand'Anse department, Haiti.

"Orpheus"
balafon, an ancient and popular West African instrument, a gourd-resonating xylophone; *bilimbao,* a type of music; *palma-christi* refers to castor oil.

"Vade Mecum"
vade mecum, Latin for a useful guidebook or document; *boula boula* is meant to evoke a racist stereotype; *Sharpeville,* a township in South Africa and site of a 1960 police massacre of anti-apartheid activists; *Guacanagaric, Anacaona,* and *Caonabo* were indigenous leaders of the island of Ayiti (later Hispaniola) at the time of Columbus's arrival, the latter two of whom resisted Spanish encroachment; *Tupac Amaru,* the 16th-century Incan leader who resisted the Spanish; *Toussaint Louverture,* prominent leader of the Haitian revolution, later kidnapped by the French and transported to the *Fort de Joux* prison in the European *Jura mountains* where he died.

"Perejil"
In the Dominican Republic, during the massacre of Haitian braceros ordered in October 1937 by the dictator Raphael Leonidas Trujillo, *perejil* was a word braceros were forced to pronounce to determine if they were Haitians or Dominicans; *bateyes,* shanty towns around sugar mills and in which cane cutters live; *viejo,* an old one, an old person.

"For You"
souï manga, Malagasy name for the Madagascar Green Sunbird.

Acknowledgments

Grateful acknowledgment is made to the editors of the following publications, who first published versions of these translations of the poems of Marie-Célie Agnant:

Asymptote: "Orpheus" (translation of "Orphée"), and "Ecstasy" (translation of "Extase")

Elektrik: Caribbean Writing: "Incandescences" (translation of "Incandescences"), "Inventory" (translation of "Inventaire"), "O my Land" (translation of "Ô ma Terre"), and "Fervent Prayer" (translation of "Jaculatoire")

Ibbetson Street: "For You" (translation of "Pour Toi")

La Machinna Sognante: "Noon" (translation of "Midi")

Mer Vox: Euménides (translation of "Euménides") and "Mother's Day" (translation of "Fete des mères")

spoKe: "Gash" (translation of "Balafre"), "Abysses" (translation of "Abîmes"), "Mimose" (translation of "Mimose"), "To My Sons" (translation of "À mes Fils"), "The Stranger" (translation of "L'étranger"), "Vade Mecum" (translation of "Vade Mecum"), "Blues for Azania" (translation of "Blues Pour L'Azanie"), "Perejil" (translation of "Perejil"), "Second Shout" (translation of "Deuxième Cri"), "Third Shout" (translation of "Troisième Cri"), "Last Shout" (translation of "Dernier Cri"), and "Brasero" (translation of "Brasero")

Grateful acknowledgment is made to Rosamond King and the editors of the Academy of American Poets' *Poem-A-Day,* who first published translated excerpts of Évelyne Trouillot's "Plidetwal."

I am indebted to the authors—Évelyne Trouillot, Marie-Célie Agnant, Maggy de Coster—for their work, as well as to the Zephyr editors, Jim Kates in particular.

I am grateful to the following institutions and individuals for their support of my work on these translations: the PEN/Heim Translation Fund, faculty members of the Boston University Program in Literary Translation; Patrick Étienne, Aziza Brathwaite Bey, Grace Cambridge, Dahlma Llanos-Figueroa, Luther Henkel, Layron Long, Jean Guerly Pétion, Patrick Romain, Martha Collins, Kevin Gallagher, Holly Guran, Daniel Bouchard, Jean-Claude Martineau, Zanset Yo, Tom Laughlin, and my Langston's Legacy workshop colleagues: Gavin Moses, Florence Ladd, Patrick Sylvain, Joshua Bennett, and Andrea Bossi.

Contributor Biographies

Évelyne Trouillot lives in Port-au-Prince, where she is a retired professor of French at the Université d'Etat d'Haiti. She is the author of eight novels, four collections of short stories, two volumes of stories for children, four books of poems, and an award-winning play. She is a member of one of Haiti's most fertile intellectual and literary families, standing alongside her siblings: novelist Lyonel Trouillot; anthropologist, historian, and political scientist Michel-Rolph Trouillot; and Kreyòl scholar and children's book author Jocelyne Trouillot. She is the co-founder of Pré-Texte, a writer's organization that sponsors reading and writing workshops.

Marie-Célie Agnant is a writer, translator, and activist whose novels have been widely-translated and include *The Book of Emma* (2004) which evokes the hardships endured by enslaved women in the Caribbean and the challenges to giving voice to this history today. Living in Montréal and writing across literary genres, she has produced poetry, fiction, and books for young readers. She received the Prix Alain-Grandbois of the Academie des Lettres du Quebec in 2017 for her most recent collection of poetry, *Femmes des terres brûlées* (2016). Her critically-acclaimed work offers poignant refusals of silence. She worked with Bread and Puppet Theatre and regularly visits Vermont. In 2023, Agnant was appointed the Canadian Parliamentary Poet Laureate.

Maggy de Coster is a poet, novelist, and translator who lives in Paris. As a journalist, she has worked for *Journal de l'Ariège* and other European and international newspapers. She is the author of more than thirty-four books in a variety of genres. Her distinctions include the 2024 Association Apulivre award for a commitment to poetry and culture. She founded the association *Manoir des Poètes*, and her poems have been translated into ten languages.

Danielle Legros Georges is a poet, translator, and editor whose work has been supported by fellowships and grants from organizations including the American Antiquarian Society, the Massachusetts Museum of Contemporary Art, the Massachusetts Cultural Council, the Boston Foundation, the PEN/Heim Translation Fund, and the Black Metropolis Research Consortium. Appointed Boston's Poet Laureate in 2014, she served in the role for four years. Her books of poetry include *The Dear Remote Nearness of You* (Barrow Street, 2016); *Island Heart,* translations of the poems of 20th-century Haitian-French poet Ida Faubert (Subpress, 2021); *Wheatley at 250: Black Women Poets Re-imagine the Verse of Phillis Wheatley Peters* (Pangyrus, 2023); and *Three Leaves, Three Roots: Poems on the Haiti-Congo Story* (Beacon Press, 2025).